"*Glorification* marries brevity and breadth
tute, highly accessible, and sharply focused t
a young student's theological horizon and re
the veteran pastor. A true pastor-theologian,
word, graciously conversant with biblical an
concerned that we know the glory of God."

  Douglas Webster, Professor of Pastoral Theology, Beeson Divinity School,
  Samford University

"This valuable series aims to be simple but not simplistic. Graham Cole's volume *Glorification* certainly achieves this. The relevant issues are convincingly discussed within a perceptive outline of the traditional doctrine, and the glorification of believers is viewed in the wider contexts of God's glory, creation glory, and future cosmic glory. Highly recommended."

  Peter Adam, Vicar Emeritus, St. Jude's Carlton; Former Principal, Ridley
  College, Melbourne

"Graham Cole has given us a brilliant introduction to the doctrine of glorification. Each chapter is grounded in Scripture and informed by key thinkers, ancient and modern. Readers will find serious engagement with the individual, corporate, and cosmic aspects of glorification as Cole offers encouragement in God's wise and glorious plan for his people."

  David S. Dockery, Distinguished Professor of Theology, Southwestern
  Baptist Theological Seminary; President, International Alliance for
  Christian Education

"An old saw claims that some people are so heavenly minded they are of no earthly good. But today most Christians seem to be so earthly minded they are of no heavenly good. In this delightful volume, Graham Cole overcomes this eclipse of heaven by masterfully rehearsing God's grand plan to glorify himself and pastorally reminding us that our chief end is to glorify God and enjoy him *forever*."

  C. Ben Mitchell, Graves Professor Emeritus of Moral Philosophy, Union
  University

"The Bible's storyline can be considered from many angles. In this resplendent volume, Graham Cole traces the neglected theme of the glory of God. Remarkably comprehensive, *Glorification* ties together many central doctrines, including the Trinity, humanity, salvation, sanctification, and eschatology. The God of the Bible is glorious, and he shares his glory with us, both now and in the future. An enlightening, edifying, and encouraging read."

  Brian S. Rosner, Principal, Ridley College, Melbourne

"Graham Cole guides us through the neglected but precious biblical theme of glorification. The glorious God who created us to bear his image saves us, uniting us to Christ, conforming us into his image, and even sharing his glory with us. Reading *Glorification* not only deepens our theology; it compels us to rejoice in our glorious God and his gifts to us, especially our glorious purpose, our glorious identity, and our glorious future."

> **Christopher W. Morgan,** Dean of the School of Christian Ministries and Professor of Theology, California Baptist University

"Glorification is not merely one of many biblical themes. As Graham Cole compellingly argues, it is a one-word summary of the whole biblical story. The Creator God has in Christ begun—and is through the Spirit continuing—to complete a building project drawn up before the foundation of the world: the creation of a cosmos and a human community that would reflect God's own glory. Why is there something rather than nothing? To communicate God's greatness. This is the Christlike vocation in which the redeemed already participate and for which they continue to hope. Glorious!"

> **Kevin Vanhoozer,** Research Professor of Systematic Theology, Trinity Evangelical Divinity School

"Graham Cole is a superb theologian, and he has given us here a much-needed overview, at once succinct and profound, of the biblical doctrine of glorification. I gladly recommend this volume to God's people everywhere."

> **Timothy George,** Distinguished Professor of Divinity, Beeson Divinity School, Samford University

"There has been a gap among evangelicals in writing about the wonderful and beautiful truth of glorification. This excellent book fills that gap. Grounding this doctrine in the divine glory of God, Cole keeps his finger in the text of Scripture and his eye on the edification of the believer. For believers, sanctification is glorification begun, while glorification is sanctification complete. In this exceptional book, we are reminded that God's promises for glorification are sure and certain—the Lord who began a good work in you will bring it to completion in God's glorious presence!"

> **Gregory C. Strand,** Executive Director of Theology and Credentialing, Evangelical Free Church of America; Adjunct Professor of Pastoral Theology, Trinity Evangelical Divinity School

Glorification

Glorification

An Introduction

Graham A. Cole

WHEATON, ILLINOIS

Trade paperback ISBN: 978-1-4335-6955-5
ePub ISBN: 978-1-4335-6958-6
PDF ISBN: 978-1-4335-6956-2
Mobipocket ISBN: 978-1-4335-6957-9

Library of Congress Cataloging-in-Publication Data

Names: Cole, Graham A. (Graham Arthur), 1949– author. | Martin, Oren R., editor.
Title: Glorification : an introduction / Graham A. Cole.
Description: Wheaton, Illinois : Crossway, 2022. | Series: Short studies in systematic theology | Includes bibliographical references and index.
Identifiers: LCCN 2021044916 (print) | LCCN 2021044917 (ebook) | ISBN 9781433569555 (trade paperback) | ISBN 9781433569562 (pdf) | ISBN 9781433569579 (mobipocket) | ISBN 9781433569586 (epub)
Subjects: LCSH: Glory of God—Christianity.
Classification: LCC BT180.G6 C65 2022 (print) | LCC BT180.G6 (ebook) | DDC 242/.2—dc23
LC record available at https://lccn.loc.gov/2021044916
LC ebook record available at https://lccn.loc.gov/2021044917

Contents

Series Preface

The ancient Greek thinker Heraclitus reputedly said that the thinker has to listen to the essence of things. A series of theological studies dealing with the traditional topics that make up systematic theology needs to do just that. Accordingly, in each of these studies, a theologian addresses the essence of a doctrine. This series thus aims to present short studies in theology that are attuned to both the Christian tradition and contemporary theology in order to equip the church to faithfully understand, love, teach, and apply what God has revealed in Scripture about a variety of topics. What may be lost in comprehensiveness can be gained through what John Calvin, in the dedicatory epistle of his commentary on Romans, called "lucid brevity."

Of course, a thorough study of any doctrine will be longer rather than shorter, as there are two millennia of confession, discussion, and debate with which to interact. As a result, a short study needs to be more selective but deftly so. Thankfully, the contributors to this series have the ability to be brief yet accurate. The key aim is that the simpler is not to morph into the simplistic. The test is whether the topic of a short study, when further studied in depth, requires some unlearning to take place. The simple can be amplified. The simplistic needs to be corrected. As editors, we believe that the volumes in this series pass that test.

While the specific focus varies, each volume (1) introduces the doctrine, (2) sets it in context, (3) develops it from Scripture, (4) draws the various threads together, and (5) brings it to bear on the Christian life. It is our prayer, then, that this series will assist the church to delight in her triune God by thinking his thoughts—which he has graciously revealed in his written word, which testifies to his living Word, Jesus Christ—after him in the powerful working of his Spirit.

Graham A. Cole and Oren R. Martin

Introduction

Thinking about the future can be daunting for many people. This is true when thinking of oneself. Will I marry? Will I have children? Will I have good health? Will I find satisfying work? Is the best ahead of me or have I passed it already? Is there life after death? If so, what does it look like?

Not long ago, I received a late-night phone call from a man who had recently turned forty. A friend of his a little older than him had just died suddenly from a heart attack. The caller was in tears. This was his first friend of around his age who had died. Now he was not only grieving but also confronting his own mortality.

Thoughts about one's future can be influenced by the society in which one lives. I have lived in three countries: Australia, the United States, and England. I found optimism about the future in both Australia and the United States, but pessimism in England. The English people I lived among seemed to have a sense of a great empire now lost and never to be recovered. In other words, a glorious past was gone forever.

Those interested in scientific scenarios about the future of the universe can also find the latest theories demoralizing. Is a coming generation going to face the heat death of the universe or the big crunch or the big chill? In any of these contemporary scientific scenarios, humankind won't survive. Over a century ago, when the heat death of the universe was commonly held as the best science, philosopher Bertrand Russell argued that in that light, "Only within the scaffolding of these truths [as claimed by the science of his day], only on the firm foundation of unyielding despair, can the soul's habitation henceforth be safely built."[1]

However, for the Christian, the best is yet to be. To rework the Russell quote: "Only within the scaffolding of these truths [as revealed in Scripture about the future], only on the firm foundation of unyielding hope, can the soul's habitation henceforth be safely built." The scriptural testimony addresses questions about the future at three levels. It speaks of the future for the individual, the future for the church, and the future of the universe.

In systematic theology, matters of the future—our hope—are covered by eschatology (Greek, *eschata*, "last things"). Traditionally this coverage has canvased two subtopics. Individual eschatology looks at the future for the individual in terms of death, judgment, and heaven or hell ("the four last things").[2] Cosmic eschatology examines ideas about the future of the universe. I suggested above that a third element needs to be considered in the light of the biblical witness: the church as the bride of Christ has a glorious future, and so there is a corporate aspect.

The purpose of this work is to examine one of the aspects of individual eschatology in the light of Scripture:[3] the doctrine

1. Bertrand Russell, "A Free Man's Worship," *The Independent Review* 1 (Dec. 1903): 416, Bertrand Russell Society (website), https://users.drew.edu/~jlenz/brs.html, accessed June 6, 2019.

2. Anthony C. Thiselton offers the valuable observation that the New Testament writers' greatest interest in last things pertains not to the four last things from the perspective of the individual "but to *the great last acts of God*, namely, the Return of Christ in glory, the resurrection of the dead, and the Last Judgment." *Life after Death: A New Approach to the Last Things* (Grand Rapids, MI: Eerdmans, 2012), xii, original emphasis. He also observes, though, that the individual's future is of "pressing concern" (xii).

3. In a work of evangelical systematic theology, Scripture as the normative word of God provides the source of the idea of glorification and the testing instrument of claims

of glorification.[4] In biblical perspective, we shall be glorified beings.[5] I was surprised to find that when I explored this doctrine, the last evangelical monograph to address glorification specifically was that by Bernard Ramm, *Them He Glorified: A Systematic Study of the Doctrine of Glorification*, published in 1963. Back then, he lamented, "I found no book which systematically explored the doctrine."[6] Here is a lacuna or gap I hope to fill by this brief study. In so doing, some aspects of both corporate and cosmic eschatology will also make their appearance.

In chapter 1, we examine the doctrine of God in terms of the divine glory. In so doing, the chapter follows the biblical plotline and its testimony to the glorious nature of God as rendered in the Old and New Testaments. Several landmarks will figure prominently in the discussion: the theophany which Moses experienced on Mount Sinai (Ex. 33–34), the prophet Isaiah's vision of the temple (Isa. 6), the prophet Ezekiel's vision of the divine chariot while in exile in Babylon (Ezek. 1), the incarnation of the Word (John 1), the transfiguration of Jesus (Mark 9), Paul's encounter with the risen Christ on the road to Damascus (Acts 9), and the end-time picture of the glory of God and the Lamb in the new earth (Rev. 21).

about glorification. Hence, there will be much appeal to passages of Scripture in this work. It follows an evidence-based method, and Scripture provides the evidence.

4. For a full-orbed discussion of the Bible's teaching on the afterlife that interacts not only with the Old and New Testaments but also with intertestamental literature, see the fine work of Paul R. Williamson, *Death and the Afterlife: Biblical Perspectives on Ultimate Questions* (Downers Grove, IL: IVP Academic, 2018).

5. Michael Horton writes, "This future hope is what theology identifies as *glorification.*" *The Christian Faith: A Systematic Theology for Pilgrims on the Way* (Grand Rapids, MI: Zondervan, 2011), 688, original emphasis.

6. Bernard Ramm, *Them He Glorified: A Systematic Study of the Doctrine of Glorification* (Grand Rapids, MI: Eerdmans, 1963), 5.

The God of biblical revelation is glorious. Eric L. Mascall appreciates this revelation when he writes, "Only if we recognize that the God of Christianity is a God of utter glory and splendor can we understand the intensity and concentration with which, down the ages, men and women have sought union with him."[7] The startling biblical truth is that this God shares his glory with us.

The glorious God of biblical revelation has a project. Chapter 2 explores this divine project, which includes bringing God's children to glory (Heb. 2:10). In the light of the great rupture delineated in Genesis 3, God has a plan to reclaim and restore his divine image bearers to himself. Divine love motivates the plan. Divine glory is the ultimate goal of the plan. To be restored to the divine image is to become a glorious being.

Understanding Romans 8:30 constitutes an important part of the chapter. The apostle wrote, "For those whom he foreknew he also predestined to be conformed to the image of his Son, in order that he might be the firstborn among many brothers. And those whom he predestined he also called, and those whom he called he also justified, and those whom he justified he also glorified" (Rom. 8:29–30). Traditionally, this so-called golden chain of redemption is all about soteriology, as the phrase implies. However, recently New Testament scholar Haley Goranson Jacob has argued that Paul is writing not about salvation but about our restoration to the glorious role of being co-regents with Christ here and now. Being glorified, according to her, is about vocation, not salvation. We participate in this vocation through our union with Christ. Is she right? We will consider her argument.

7. E. L. Mascall, *The Christian Universe* (London: Darton, Longman and Todd, 1966), 57.

Chapter 3 addresses the matter of the glorification experienced in this life. Paul is our guide. He wrote to the Corinthians about how the Spirit transforms us from one degree of glory to another (2 Cor. 3:18). Is this a passive process where God does all the work, or do we share in the process? How does this process relate to our sanctification? These questions and others are dealt with in this chapter.

Chapter 4 explores the prospect of glory. Hope is vital to the Christian life. Our eschatological horizon is so very different to that of the secularist. The prospect is of nothing less than a new heaven and a new earth, for which the groaning creation is longing, and with it the revealing of the glorious liberty of the children of God (Rom. 8:18–25). The sphere of glory to come requires the transformation of our bodies (1 Cor. 15:44). Our bodies need to become like that of Christ's own glorified body (Phil. 3:20–21). The nature of the glorified body will be explored, as will the question of when that body is received. Aspects of both corporate and cosmic eschatology will also figure in the discussion.

Chapter 5 deals with the question Who will be glorified? C. S. Lewis saw the implications of the hope of glory when he wrote:

> It is a serious thing to live in a society of possible gods and goddesses, to remember that the dullest and most uninteresting person you can talk to may one day be a creature which, if you saw it now, you would be strongly tempted to worship, or else a horror and a corruption such as you now meet, if at all, only in a nightmare. All day long we are, in some degree, helping each other to one or other of these destinations. It is in the light of these overwhelming possibilities, it is with the awe and the circumspection proper to them, that we should conduct all our dealings with one

another, all friendships, all loves, all play, all politics. There are no *ordinary* people. You have never talked to a mere mortal. Nations, cultures, arts, civilizations—these are mortal, and their life is to ours as the life of a gnat. But it is immortals whom we joke with, work with, marry, snub, and exploit—immortal horrors or everlasting splendours.[8]

Will these "everlasting splendours" only be those who trust in Christ? Such a notion suggests an exclusivity that would make secularists bristle.

But what about those whom Lewis describes as "immortal horrors"? We will explore the traditional view of what that means as well as the speculative suggestions of Lewis and N. T. Wright. What would embodied existence look like when excluded from the divine presence? is an interesting question. However, we need to distinguish carefully between biblically anchored convictions, opinions that are less so, and speculations that have little anchorage in the biblical testimony. Even so, in the end, some may turn out to be true.

A brief summarizing conclusion rounds out this study, together with some further reading suggestions for those readers who want to go deeper.

---

8. C. S. Lewis, *Screwtape Proposes a Toast and Other Pieces* (London and Glasgow: Fontana, 1969), 109, original emphasis.

1

Our Glorious God

In this chapter, we explore the concept of the divine glory. To do so, we examine the biblical testimony to the glorious nature of God as revealed in the Old and New Testaments. To drill deeper, we then focus on selected biblical passages dealing with glory before turning our attention to an intriguing question of divine glory and the divine attributes. Considering the divine glory is germane to this study of glorification because, according to 2 Corinthians 3:18, we are to reflect the divine glory as we are transformed from one degree of glory to the next.[1]

The Concept of Glory

We access concepts through words and how they are used. According to Leslie C. Allen, "In secular usage, the Hebrew word for

1. Both the ESV and the NIV have "reflect[ing] the glory of the Lord" in a footnote, while the NLT has both the idea of seeing and reflecting in the main text: "So all of us who have had that veil removed can see and reflect the glory of the Lord. And the Lord—who is the Spirit—makes us more and more like him as we are changed into his glorious image." For a brief discussion of the translation issues, see Thomas A. Smail, *Reflected Glory: The Spirit in Christ and Christians* (London: Hodder and Stoughton, 1975), 25.

glory [*kabod*] . . . primarily means 'weight,' referring to something substantial as in Isaiah 22:24." There Isaiah writes of how God will honor Eliakim, the son of Hilkiah, as the new royal steward: "And they will hang on him the whole honor [*kabod*] of his father's house, the offspring and issue, every small vessel, from the cups to all the flagons." L. C. Allen rightly suggests that in this Isaianic context, "the term connotes honor and fame as coming from a social status that includes greatness, wealth, or power, and the acknowledgment of others."[2] Interestingly, the first use of *kabod* in the Old Testament has a very human context. Jacob hears what the sons of Laban are accusing him of doing. In Genesis 31:1 we read, "Jacob has taken all that was our father's, and from what was our father's he has gained all his wealth [*kabod*]." When used of God, as in the phrase "the glory of the Lord," it becomes almost a technical expression of the majesty, weightiness, even beauty of God.[3] In the Greek Old Testament (the Septuagint, or LXX), the word used to translate the Hebrew term for glory (*doxa*) accented the ideas of honor, reputation, and praise.[4] Glory and divine kingship are connected, as Haley Goranson Jacob argues in light of the Septuagint: "God's glory is commonly associated with his status or identity as king."[5] In the biblical writings, various phenomena are associated with the divine glory: shining light (Num. 6:25); thunder, brightness, fire, and beauty (Ex. 24:16–17; Ps. 29:3); and clouds (Mark 14:62).[6] The New Testament writers also commonly

2. L. C. Allen, "Glory," in *The Lexham Bible Dictionary*, ed. John D. Barry et al. (Bellingham, WA: Lexham, 2016), Logos Bible Software.

3. Richard B. Gaffin Jr., "Glory," in *New Dictionary of Biblical Theology*, ed. T. Desmond Alexander and Brian S. Rosner (Downers Grove, IL: InterVarsity Press, 2000), 507–11.

4. G. B. Caird argues, "Whatever their reasons, they [the LXX translators] chose *doxa* to represent *kabod* in almost all its occurrences." *The Language and Imagery of the Bible* (London: Duckworth, 1980), 77.

5. Haley Goranson Jacob, *Conformed to the Image of His Son: Reconsidering Paul's Theology of Glory in Romans* (Downers Grove, IL: IVP Academic, 2018), 42.

6. See Anthony C. Thiselton, *Life after Death: A New Approach to the Last Things* (Grand Rapids, MI: Eerdmans, 2012), 192. According to Thiselton, "During the Intertestamental period the rabbis and Judaism spoke of God's glory as the Shekinah, although

used *doxa* when referring to the divine glory.[7] In both the Old and the New Testaments, this glory is "visible splendor," as Richard Bauckham points out.[8]

In his classic essay on the plan of God, J. I. Packer captures the Old Testament thrust well: "The term 'glory' thus connects the thoughts of God's praiseworthiness and of His praise—of the majesty of the revelation of His power and presence from which religion springs, and of the worship which is the right response when we realise that God stands before us, and we before Him."[9]

In modern parlance, the concept of glory has some overlap with the biblical understanding of glory. We hear news commentators speak of Olympic glory when an athlete wins a gold medal, or we read of those pursuing academic glory in their schooling. The concept is one of honor, renown, admiration, and recognition. Such achievements bring glory, and others rightly recognize those achievements. So we celebrate our Olympians and give scholarships to valedictorians.

Some Key Passages

To explore all the relevant texts and significant moments in redemptive history concerning divine glory would require a book in itself. For our purposes, some key passages, key events, key institutions, and key personages will be considered.[10] These include celebrating God's glory (Ps. 19), God's

---

this is not a biblical term" (192). *Shekinah* is the transliteration of a Hebrew word meaning "dwelling" or "settling." It is understood in this usage that the divine glory is that which dwells in a space or settles on something (e.g., the tabernacle and the temple).

7. Caird, *Language and Imagery*, 78.

8. Richard Bauckham, *Gospel of Glory: Major Themes in Johannine Theology* (Grand Rapids, MI: Baker Academic, 2015), 44.

9. J. I. Packer, *The Plan of God*, https://www.the-highway.com/, accessed June 28, 2019.

10. Christopher W. Morgan, "Toward a Theology of the Glory of God," in *The Glory of God*, ed. Christopher W. Morgan and Robert A. Peterson (Wheaton, IL: Crossway, 2010), 155. Morgan provides an excellent survey of the key passages and junctures in the history of redemption that are testimony to the glory of God.

glory and our own (Ps. 8), God's triumph in defeating Pharaoh's forces (Ex. 15), the theophany on Sinai (Ex. 24:15–17; 33–34; 40:34–35), the theophany in the temple (Isa. 6), the chariot of cherubim (Ezek. 1), the incarnation (John 1), the transfiguration of Jesus (Mark 9; 2 Pet. 1), Paul's encounter with the risen Christ on the road to Damascus (Acts 9), and the final eschatological picture found in the last book in the canon of Scripture (Rev. 21).

Creation

In Psalm 19, the psalmist knows that he worships a glorious God, for creation in all its beauty tells him that. He sings:

> The heavens declare the glory of God,
> and the sky above proclaims his handiwork.
> Day to day pours out speech,
> and night to night reveals knowledge. (vv. 1–2)

Exhibit A for the psalmist is the majestic sun,

> which comes out like a bridegroom leaving his
> chamber,
> and, like a strong man, runs its course with joy.
> Its rising is from the end of the heavens,
> and its circuit to the end of them,
> and there is nothing hidden from its heat. (vv. 5–6)

Tremper Longman comments:

> Even to the ancients, who did not have an awareness of the actual vastness of the heavens or the size of the sun, moon and stars, the skies gave a sense of transcendence, of someone above themselves. Even today, with all of modern science's descriptions and explanations, it is not

rare for us to have our minds stunned by God's incredible creation.[11]

The ancients did not have telescopes, so to the naked eye the sun was the biggest celestial object and therefore a fitting object to make the point about God's glory.[12]

Humankind

Psalm 8 appears to be a reflection on Genesis 1 put to song. It begins and ends on the note of the divine majesty (vv. 1, 9). The use of the same words at the beginning and end of a passage is known, in literary terms, as an *inclusio*, and it shows what the psalm is about: namely, God's majesty:

> O LORD, our Lord,
>> how majestic is your name in all the earth!

God's glory, though, is not lost sight of: "You have set your glory above the heavens" (v. 1). The grandeur of the heavens and moon seem to make humankind so insignificant (vv. 3–4). So why should the glorious God have a care for this creature? The answer lies in God's giving humans a royal role:

> Yet you have made him a little lower than the heavenly
>> beings
>> and crowned him with glory and honor.
> You have given him dominion over the works of your
>> hands;
>> you have put all things under his feet. (vv. 5–6)

11. T. Longman III, *Psalms: An Introduction and Commentary*, Tyndale Old Testament Commentaries (Nottingham: Inter-Varsity Press, 2014), 188.

12. The biblical writers described the natural world in terms of what could be seen. Even today, we speak of the sun's rising and setting, although we know from astronomy that the reality is different. The philosophical term for the biblical approach is "phenomenological."

The sphere of dominion, which covers the heavens, the earth, and the seas, includes

> all sheep and oxen,
>> and also the beasts of the field,
> the birds of the heavens, and the fish of the sea,
>> whatever passes along the paths of the seas. (vv. 7–8)

The echoes of the Genesis story are clear. What also is clear is the value that the Creator places on this particular creature. Elmer Martens expresses this point in a provocative way: "If one were to imagine a scale of 1 to 10, with living creatures such as beasts as 1 and God as 10, then so high is the writer's estimation of humanity, he should have to put him at 8 or 9. It is God, and not animals, who is man's closest relative."[13]

The Exodus

God's mighty acts delineated in Scripture are more than creative ones. God not only creates; he also saves and judges. The story of the exodus of God's people from Egypt shows both motifs, especially in the song Moses sang in the light of the defeat of Pharaoh's pursuing army:

> I will sing to the LORD, for he has triumphed gloriously;
>> the horse and his rider he has thrown into the sea
>>> [God judges].
> The LORD is my strength and my song,
>> and he has become my salvation [God saves];
> this is my God, and I will praise him,
>> my father's God, and I will exalt him. (Ex. 15:1–2)

13. Elmer Martens, quoted in Bruce K. Waltke, James M. Houston, and Erika Moore, *The Psalms as Christian Worship: A Historical Commentary* (Grand Rapids, MI: Eerdmans, 2010), 269.

There is no God in the ancient Near East like this God, as Moses's question shows when he says:

> Who is like you, O LORD, among the gods?
>> Who is like you, majestic in holiness,
>> awesome in glorious deeds, doing wonders?
>>> (Ex. 15:11)

There is only one divine King: "The LORD will reign forever and ever" (Ex. 15:18). As John I. Durham points out, "The poem of Exodus 15 celebrates Yahweh present *with* his people and doing *for* them as no other god anywhere and at any time *can* be present to do."[14]

The importance of this Old Testament event is shown by Miriam's response. She teaches Moses's song to the women who have experienced the divine rescue:

> And Miriam sang to them:
>
>> "Sing to the LORD, for he has triumphed gloriously;
>> the horse and his rider he has thrown into the sea."
>>> (Ex. 15:21)

Douglas K. Stuart comments:

> Moses had authored this great victory song; Miriam now popularized it among all the women so that it would be known and sung in every family, every home. The result was that every Israelite, whether descended from Abraham or newly joined to the nation (12:38) would know by heart the story of the great divine deliverance of God's people at the sea.[15]

14. John I. Durham, *Exodus*, Word Biblical Commentary (Dallas: Word, 1987), 210.

15. Douglas K. Stuart, *Exodus*, The New American Commentary (Nashville: Broadman & Holman, 2006), 364. Stuart argues, "The quotation of 15:1 here in v. 21 by

The exodus story was the great old covenant good news story, just as for the Christian the greater story of Jesus's coming, cross, and overcoming death is the new covenant good news story, the gospel.

The Sinai Theophany

God appeared to all his rescued people on Sinai. What a sight it was, as Exodus 24:16–17 describes: "The glory of the LORD dwelt on Mount Sinai, and the cloud covered it six days. And on the seventh day he called to Moses out of the midst of the cloud. Now the appearance of the glory of the LORD was like a devouring fire on the top of the mountain in the sight of the people of Israel." Here are the key accents of glory: divine presence, cloud, and fire.[16] Some forty years later, Moses related the people's response: "And you said, 'Behold, the LORD our God has shown us his glory and greatness, and we have heard his voice out of the midst of the fire. This day we have seen God speak with man, and man still live'" (Deut. 5:24). Clearly, the people of Israel had accurately assessed the importance of the experience and rightly categorized the Sinai experience in glory terms.

But Moses wanted more. On Sinai, he asked the Lord to show him the divine glory (Ex. 33:18). God's reply is instructive: "And he said, 'I will make all my goodness pass before you and will proclaim before you my name 'The LORD.' And I will be gracious to whom I will be gracious, and will show mercy on whom I will show mercy'" (Ex. 33:19). As I have written elsewhere: "Moses wanted glory. He wanted to see the majesty of God. Instead God gave him goodness. God's glory lies in his

---

Miriam is simply a way of saying that she taught the Israelite women the *entire* song, not just the opening words cited in v. 21" (364, original emphasis).

16. See R. A. Cole, *Exodus: An Introduction and Commentary*, Tyndale Old Testament Commentaries (Downers Grove, IL: InterVarsity Press, 1973), 195.

goodness, not his might, and that goodness is seen expressed in sovereign grace and mercy."[17]

Richard Bauckham comments insightfully on Exodus 33–34 in his treatment of the glory theme in the Johannine literature: "The story seems to suggest that God's glory is the radiance of his character, of his goodness, of who he truly is."[18] God turned Moses's request in a distinctly moral direction. God's glory resides in goodness and not in raw divine power. God did indeed make his glory pass by Moses. Moses, however, was hidden in the cleft of the rock. The sight of the divine in the face of God would have proved a terminal experience for Moses (Ex. 33:20–23). Even so, it was a dramatic experience that rightly led Moses to worship: "And Moses quickly bowed his head toward the earth and worshiped" (Ex. 34:8).

The Tabernacle

God's "walking" in the garden in Genesis 2–3 reveals his will to be present with his people, but, as Genesis 3 tragically shows, sin separates humanity from his presence. The question then becomes how a holy God can dwell with an unholy people. The answer is *in God's way, not ours*. Hence, God gives the elaborate design of the tabernacle. Exodus 25:9 says, "Exactly as I show you concerning the pattern of the tabernacle, and of all its furniture, so you shall make it." The design was followed, and so we read: "Then the cloud covered the tent of meeting, and the glory of the LORD filled the tabernacle" (Ex. 40:34). R. A. Cole offers this observation:

> Two thoughts are joined in this chapter [Ex. 40]. The first is that God shows his approval of the completed work by

17. Graham A. Cole, "Exodus 34, the Middoth and the Doctrine of God: The Importance of Biblical Theology to Evangelical Systematic Theology," *Southern Baptist Journal of Theology* 12, no. 3 (2008): 27.
18. Bauckham, *Gospel of Glory*, 50.

descending in the cloud of "glory" that shows his presence (cf. 33:9). Indeed, he so covers and fills the tent that now not even Moses, God's faithful servant (Num. 12:7), dares to enter ([Ex. 40] verse 35). The second allied thought is that this same cloud, the symbol of the presence of YHWH, led the way by day and night all through the desert years of Israel's experience (verse 36).[19]

The holy God has come to dwell in the midst of his people.

The Failure in the Wilderness

God's old covenant people rebelled in the wilderness at multiple points, despite the exodus and the theophany on Sinai. One such occasion was the reaction of the people to the report of the spies. Canaan, according to the majority report, to which Caleb and Joshua took exception, was full of doom if Israel entered the promised land. So the people hankered for a return to the land of their bondage: "And they said to one another, 'Let us choose a leader and go back to Egypt'" (Num. 14:4). Moses interceded for Israel, and the divine response was merciful: "Then the LORD said, 'I have pardoned, according to your [Moses's] word'" (Num. 14:20). And yet, there were consequences for persistent rebellion:

> But truly, as I live, and as all the earth shall be filled with the glory of the LORD, none of the men who have seen my glory and my signs that I did in Egypt and in the wilderness, and yet have put me to the test these ten times and have not obeyed my voice, shall see the land that I swore to give to their fathers. And none of those who despised me shall see it. (Num. 14:21–23)

19. Cole, *Exodus*, 248–49.

Glory was coming, but the wilderness rebels wouldn't see it.[20] Why should they? They had witnessed it in the mighty deeds of God but did not take it to heart. Psalm 95 sums it up:

Today, if you hear his voice,
> do not harden your hearts, as at Meribah,
> as on the day at Massah in the wilderness,
when your fathers put me to the test
> and put me to the proof, though they had seen my
>> work. (vv. 7–9)

As Gordon J. Wenham notes, "The divine pardon does not mean Israel will escape all punishment for their sin, only that they will not suffer the total annihilation they deserve."[21]

The Temple Vision

The prophet Isaiah was granted an overwhelming vision of the divine glory: "In the year that King Uzziah died I saw the Lord sitting upon a throne, high and lifted up; and the train of his robe filled the temple" (Isa. 6:1). Isaiah experienced not only a theophany but also an angelophany: "Above him stood the seraphim. Each had six wings: with two he covered his face, and with two he covered his feet, and with two he flew" (Isa. 6:2).[22] The seraphim (throne angels) were not silent:

And one called to another and said:

> "Holy, holy, holy is the LORD of hosts;
> the whole earth is full of his glory!" (Isa. 6:3)

---

20. Interestingly, there appears to be an age of accountability in Scripture. The "little ones" in the wilderness will enter the promised land (cf. Deut. 1:39 and Jonah 4:11).

21. Gordon I. Wenham, *Numbers: An Introduction and Commentary*, Tyndale Old Testament Commentaries (Downers Grove, IL: InterVarsity Press, 1981), 138.

22. A theophany is an appearance of God (Greek, *theos*, "God," and *phainein*, "to appear"). An angelophany is an appearance of an angel (Greek, *angelos*, "angel," and *phainein*, "to appear").

The vision brought to Isaiah a sense of uncleanness before this holy God: "And I said: 'Woe is me! For I am lost; for I am a man of unclean lips, and I dwell in the midst of a people of unclean lips; for my eyes have seen the King, the LORD of hosts!'" (Isa. 6:5). As with the Sinai theophany, there is a moral aspect to seeing the divine glory.

John's Gospel brings together the temple vision of Isaiah 6 and the suffering servant theme from Isaiah 53 by way of application to Jesus. John writes, "Isaiah said these things because he saw his glory and spoke of him" (John 12:41). Colin Kruse comments:

> Referring to the prophecy, the evangelist says, *Isaiah said this because he saw Jesus' glory and spoke about him.* The allusion is to Isaiah's vision of God in the temple and his commission to be his messenger to Israel (Isa. 6:1–13). The evangelist implies that what Isaiah saw in the temple was in fact "Jesus' glory," i.e. the glory of the pre-existent Christ.[23]

The glorious temple presence of Israel's God finds its definitive location in Jesus Christ.

Ezekiel's Visions of God

The prophet Ezekiel, some two centuries after Isaiah's vision in the temple, likewise had a vision of the glory of God (Ezek. 1:1–28). The prophet was in exile in Babylon by the Chebar canal. According to G. B. Caird:

> In 598 B.C. Ezekiel had his vision of the chariot of the cherubim with its multi-directional wheels, surmounted by a firmament on which was enthroned a figure of celestial

23. Colin G. Kruse, *John: An Introduction and Commentary*, Tyndale New Testament Commentaries (Downers Grove, IL: InterVarsity Press, 2003), 271, original emphasis. Bauckham argues similarly, *Gospel of Glory*, 53.

radiance. This he called "the glory of the Lord," and from that moment on, so influential was his vision on all who succeeded him, "radiance" became part of the connotation of *kabod*.[24]

The descriptors in the vision are striking. Here are some of them: "a stormy wind" (v. 4), "fire" (vv. 4, 13), "living creatures" (v. 5 et passim), "lightning" (vv. 13–14), "shining like awe-inspiring crystal" (v. 22), "a sound of tumult" (v. 24), and "brightness all around" (v. 28). Suffice it to say that the vision of the chariot throne of God with the four living creatures empowering it created a physical reaction in the prophet. Ezekiel 1:28 tells us: "Such was the appearance of the likeness of the glory of the LORD. And when I saw it, I fell on my face, and I heard the voice of one speaking." Lamar E. Cooper comments astutely:

> Humanity in peril needs a sense of the awesome majesty of God. There needs to be an awareness that God is greater than adversity. He is with his people in the midst of their problems. This was a need of both Ezekiel and the people to whom he ministered. They needed a new vision of and commitment to the holiness and majesty of God.[25]

The Lord gave Ezekiel that new vision of the splendid glory of God.

Ezekiel also tells of visions of the loss of divine glory. Exile came because of Judah's sin, and neither the city of Jerusalem nor its temple was an exception to the problem. In fact, Jerusalem would be destroyed because of its wickedness (Ezek. 5:5–6).

---

24. Caird, *The Language and Imagery of the Bible*, 76.
25. Lamar Eugene Cooper, *Ezekiel: An Exegetical and Theological Exposition of Holy Scripture*, The New American Commentary (Nashville: Broadman & Holman, 1994), 72.

> Thus says the Lord GOD: This is Jerusalem. I have set her
> in the center of the nations, with countries all around her.
> And she has rebelled against my rules by doing wickedness
> more than the nations, and against my statutes more than
> the countries all around her; for they have rejected my rules
> and have not walked in my statutes.

The note of rebellion is sounded more than once in the prophecy (e.g. Ezek. 12:1–3), and so too is the note of idolatry. When sin is against the divine King, rebellion is indeed the appropriate descriptor.

The temple comes in for particular condemnation. The prophet has a vison of the glory of God present in the temple (Ezek. 8:3–4). But so too is idolatry on a striking scale: "the image of jealousy," "great abominations," "idols," "weeping for Tammuz," and "worshiping the sun" (Ezek. 8:3, 6, 10, 14, 16). Cooper sums up the sad story: "The worship Ezekiel described suggested a developed program of regular pagan worship in the sanctuary that was to be exclusively for the worship of Yahweh."[26] "The image of jealousy" is a particularly intriguing reference (Ezek. 8:3). The prophet does not elaborate, presumably because the first hearers and readers knew the reference. Leslie C. Allen offers the following plausible explanation of the phrase:

> The "image" (סמל) he sees at this place is an anthropomorphic idol, to judge by the usage of the term in Phoenician inscriptions. Significantly, the same term occurs in 2 Chr 33:7, 15, seemingly with reference to the Phoenician goddess Asherah, in connection with an image set up in the temple precincts (2 Kgs 21:7). If this cult, abolished by Josiah, was revived after his death, the cult image may have been placed elsewhere (McKay, *Religion* 22–23, 93 n. 27). Here it has

26. Cooper, *Ezekiel*, 119–20.

pride of place as a guardian figure. The focus of the narrative lies in the religious significance of the image, as an outrage to Yahweh, more literally a provocation to jealousy (קנא).[27]

And so, in response to such idolatry, the glory of the divine presence departs from the temple: "Then the cherubim lifted up their wings, with the wheels beside them, and the glory of the God of Israel was over them. And the glory of the LORD went up from the midst of the city and stood on the mountain that is on the east side of the city" (Ezek. 11:22–23). Sin had consequences, and Jerusalem lost the glory of God dwelling in its midst.

However, the prophet also sees a future in which the divine glory returns. The Lord will forgive and restore his people. He won't leave them bereft of his presence forever. Ezekiel sees a new temple. In great detail, he elaborates on its structure, contents, and decoration. Importantly, the glory returns (Ezek. 43:1–5).

> Then he led me to the gate, the gate facing east. And behold, the glory of the God of Israel was coming from the east. And the sound of his coming was like the sound of many waters, and the earth shone with his glory. And the vision I saw was just like the vision that I had seen when he came to destroy the city, and just like the vision that I had seen by the Chebar canal. And I fell on my face. As the glory of the LORD entered the temple by the gate facing east, the Spirit lifted me up and brought me into the inner court; and behold, the glory of the LORD filled the temple.

As Leslie Allen points out: "In the course of that vision, Yahweh's re-entry through the east gate and the filling of the temple with his glory (43:1–5; cf. v 7) represent a wonderful reversal. Where sin abounded and judgment rightly fell, grace was to superabound in

27. Leslie C. Allen, *Ezekiel 1–19*, Word Biblical Commentary (Dallas: Word, 1994), 142.

the holy fellowship of God and his people."[28] In fact, the return of the divine glory is the necessary condition to be met for the prophecy to reach its climax in this claim: "And the name of the city from that time on shall be, The LORD Is There" (Ezek. 48:35).

The Word Made Flesh

The prologue of John's Gospel begins in eternity with the Word who is with God and is God (1:1), and climaxes with this Word becoming flesh: "And the Word became flesh and dwelt among us, and we have seen his glory, glory as of the only Son from the Father, full of grace and truth" (1:14). Richard Bauckham draws out the significance of this verse when he writes in relation to the claim "the Word became flesh and dwelt among us": "This phrase echoes the dwelling of God's glory in the tabernacle and the temple, God's gracious presence at the heart of his people's life. Now the glory in the flesh of Jesus Christ is God's tent-dwelling among his people."[29] Vaughan Roberts sums up the significance of John 1:14 more expansively:

> Adam and Eve enjoyed God's presence with them in the garden before the fall. God also drew near to the Israelites, living in their midst in the tabernacle and then in the temple. But the temple in Jerusalem was just a shadow of what we receive in Christ. He is the true temple, the place where we may enter perfectly into God's presence. He is not just the true human being; he is the true God. In Christ, God himself has drawn near to us.[30]

Moreover, John's reference to "grace and truth" echoes the definitive Old Testament revelation of the character of God

---

28. Allen, *Ezekiel 1–19*, 169.
29. Bauckham, *Gospel of Glory*, 51.
30. Vaughan Roberts, *God's Big Picture: Tracing the Storyline of the Bible* (Downers Grove, IL: InterVarsity Press, 2002), 118.

on Mount Sinai: the God who is gracious, merciful, and covenantally faithful (esp. Ex. 34:6–7).[31]

The incarnate Word's glory was witnessed by the disciples at the wedding at Cana when Jesus turned the water into wine: "This, the first of his signs, Jesus did at Cana in Galilee, and manifested his glory. And his disciples believed in him" (John 2:11). Yet that glory, full of grace and truth, was not immediately obvious. At first, Nicodemus, for example, saw Jesus only as "a teacher come from God" (John 3:2). The Pharisees were divided in their estimate of Jesus, as John 9:16 shows: "Some of the Pharisees said, 'This man is not from God, for he does not keep the Sabbath.' But others said, 'How can a man who is a sinner do such signs?' And there was a division among them." Clearly, not all the Pharisees were dismissive of Jesus. Again, Nicodemus serves as an example. Later in John's account, Nicodemus, together with Joseph of Arimathea, showed his devotion to Jesus by burying him according to Jewish custom (John 19:38–42).

That Jesus's glory was not evident to all should not surprise the reader of John's Gospel. John 17:5 provides the clue, one that we shall explore more fully later. Jesus prayed, "And now, Father, glorify me in your own presence with the glory that I had with you before the world existed." Clearly, Jesus forwent a glory in becoming flesh and taking the form of a servant, but would regain that glory upon his return to the Father.

The next New Testament passage we consider lifts the veil on Jesus's glory.

The Transfiguration

Accounts of the transfiguration of Jesus can be found in Matthew, Mark, and Luke. It is a stunning event. Jesus has just informed

---

31. For more on the significance of Ex. 34 for the doctrine of God, see Cole, "Exodus 34, the Middoth and the Doctrine of God," 24–36.

the disciples of his coming death on the cross. Mark's account indicates that some of those disciples will "not taste death until they see the kingdom of God" (9:1). The kingdom of God in the Gospels refers mainly to the active reign of God, rather than the realm in which it is experienced.[32] That active display of divine sovereignty seems to be the thrust of Jesus's prediction. Six days later on a high mountain, Peter, James, and John in the company of Jesus see the transfiguration of their Master (Mark 9:2). Mark tells us, "And he was transfigured before them, and his clothes became radiant, intensely white, as no one on earth could bleach them" (9:3–4).[33] Matthew adds that Jesus's "face shone like the sun" (17:2). Luke expands the picture and does so in glory terms: "Now Peter and those who were with him were heavy with sleep, but when they became fully awake they saw his glory and the two men [Moses and Elijah] who stood with him" (9:32). According to Matthew and Mark, the sight of the transfigured Christ terrifies the disciples (Matt. 17:6; Mark 9:6).

Years later, Peter reflects on his experience when writing to fellow believers. He makes it clear that the story of the transfiguration is not a historical fiction but comes from firsthand experience: "For we did not follow cleverly devised myths when we made known to you the power and coming of our Lord Jesus Christ, but we were eyewitnesses of his majesty" (2 Pet. 1:16). How then did he understand what happened to Jesus on the mountain? Second Peter 1:17–18 tells us: "For when he received honor and glory from God the Father, and the voice was borne to him by the Majestic Glory, 'This is my beloved Son, with whom I am well pleased,' we ourselves heard this

32. For a text that refers to the reign of God on display, see Luke 11:20 (exorcisms), and for one that speaks of the realm that can be entered, see Matt. 5:20.

33. The reference to "six days" is unusually specific in Mark's account of Jesus, and I see it as underlining the connection of the transfiguration event to Jesus's promise that some would see the kingdom in their lifetime. It may also be connected to Moses's six days on Sinai (Ex. 24), painting Jesus as the greater Moses with greater revelation.

very voice borne from heaven, for we were with him on the holy mountain."

The Damascus Road Encounter

Saul of Tarsus also experienced that glory, and that event changed his life and the trajectory of Christianity. This once-violent man and, by his own admission, persecutor of the church would become the apostle to the Gentiles who could subsequently write the most profound statement on love to be found in any literature (cf. Phil. 3:6; 1 Tim. 1:13 and 1 Cor. 13). He was on the road to Damascus with a mission. The book of Acts relates the story: "But Saul, still breathing threats and murder against the disciples of the Lord, went to the high priest and asked him for letters to the synagogues at Damascus, so that if he found any belonging to the Way, men or women, he might bring them bound to Jerusalem" (9:1–2). Then the unexpected happened: "Now as he went on his way, he approached Damascus, and suddenly a light from heaven shone around him" (Acts 9:3). The risen Christ had a question for Saul: "And falling to the ground, he heard a voice saying to him, 'Saul, Saul, why are you persecuting me?'" (Acts 9:4). Blinded by the light, he had his own question to ask: "And he said, 'Who are you, Lord?' And he said, 'I am Jesus, whom you are persecuting'" (Acts 9:5).

Twice more in Acts, Saul, now Paul, recounts what happened to him. He references the brightness of the light and that it came from heaven (cf. 22:11 and 26:13). The word "glory" is not in these conversion accounts, but the language of light and brightness is the key to our recognizing glory's presence in Paul's Damascus road encounter with the risen Christ.

All Is Temple

Revelation 21, the penultimate chapter in the biblical canon, presents a remarkable prospect: "Then I saw a new heaven and a new earth, for the first heaven and the first earth had passed away, and the sea was no more. And I saw the holy city, new Jerusalem, coming down out of heaven from God, prepared as a bride adorned for her husband" (vv. 1–2).

Russell Moore captures the theological import of this revelation of the future: "The point of the gospel is not that we would go to heaven when we die. Instead, it is that heaven will come down, transforming, and renewing the earth and the entire universe."[34] Fascinatingly, the new Jerusalem is cubical in shape, and the only other cubical space in Scripture is the Most Holy Place in the tabernacle and temple. The theological import of this rich symbolism is that the new earth is now all sacred temple space replete with the glorious presence of God and the Lamb. Hence, John says: "And I saw no temple in the city, for its temple is the Lord God the Almighty and the Lamb. And the city has no need of sun or moon to shine on it, for the glory of God gives it light, and its lamp is the Lamb" (Rev. 21:22–23). Once again, we see the nexus between glory and light.

Christopher W. Morgan rightly points out that every section of Scripture speaks of the glory of God: "Law, Prophets, Writings, Gospels, Acts, Pauline Epistles, General Epistles, and Revelation."[35] (Only in John's letters is there no reference to God's glory per se.) This is remarkable. The pervasiveness of the glory of God theme in both the Old and the New Testaments testifies to its importance.

An Intriguing Question

The divine attributes are commonly grouped into two categories: the incommunicable attributes and the communicable attributes of God. Aseity, an incommunicable attribute, asserts that only God is

---

34. Russell D. Moore, "Personal and Cosmic Eschatology," in *A Theology for the Church*, ed. Daniel L. Akin, rev. ed. (Nashville: B&H, 2014), 711; a splendid volume.
35. Morgan, "Toward a Theology of the Glory of God," 154.

self-existent. God relies on nothing and no one outside himself to exist. No other being has aseity; only God has life in himself. Communicable attributes are those that can be attributed to both God and us, though with God there is a perfection we do not share. For example, God loves and we too can love, albeit imperfectly.

Is glory an attribute of God? Bruce Milne argues so. He makes glory the beginning point of his enumeration of the divine attributes. Milne writes: "His glory carries us to the heart of all that is essential to his being as God, his divine majesty, his sheer *God*ness."[36] Bernard Ramm also maintains that glory is a divine attribute but states it differently than Milne: "The glory of God is not, however, a particularized attribute like the wisdom of God but an attribute of the total nature of God, virtually an attribute of attributes."[37] In its exaggeration Ramm's affirmation lacks nuance and, for some, may raise questions about divine simplicity. Herman Bavinck is much more careful: "The 'glory of the Lord' is the splendor and brilliance that is inseparably associated with all God's attributes and his self-revelation in nature and grace."[38]

Christopher Morgan argues that glory can refer to "a summary of attributes of God,"[39] which means glory sums up both the incommunicable and communicable attributes of God in some way. This argument has merit. The God of the Bible is gloriously self-existent, gloriously omnipotent, gloriously omniscient, gloriously holy, gloriously loving, and so on. The divine glory also has an aesthetic aspect. It is beautiful. Yet as Bernard Ramm, in his discussion of glory and beauty in the light of the

36. Bruce Milne, *Know the Truth: A Handbook of Christian Belief* (Downers Grove, IL: InterVarsity Press, 2009), 85, original emphasis of half of the word. Although Milne distinguishes the communicable from the incommunicable attributes, he does not apply the distinction to the elaboration of the attributes.

37. Bernard Ramm, *Them He Glorified: A Systematic Study of the Doctrine of Glorification* (Grand Rapids, MI: Eerdmans, 1963), 18.

38. Herman Bavinck, *Reformed Dogmatics: Abridged in One Volume*, ed. John Bolt (Grand Rapids, MI: Baker Academic, 2011), 215.

39. Morgan, *The Glory of God*, 157.

biblical evidence, wisely maintains, "The notion that God is beautiful is not a leading biblical notion but a secondary one. The primary focus of Scripture is on the glory of God as such, the aesthetic motif being purely secondary."[40]

Conclusion

The God of the Bible can be described in many ways that are faithful to the biblical text: all-holy, almighty, all-wise, all-good, and all-knowing. The living God is also all-glorious: The Father is glorious; the Son is glorious, and the Spirit is glorious. The triune God is unimaginably splendid. The divine splendor has a moral dimension, as the theophany on Sinai showed and Isaiah experienced in the temple. "Goodness" can be a synonym for "glory." However, goodness does not exhaust what divine glory is. Other descriptors are needed, such as "majesty," "splendor," "weightiness," and even "beauty." Metaphors are relevant too, such as "fire," "light," "shining," and "brightness."

The divine splendor is on display in both Old and New Testament texts as we saw in the key texts we considered. There is thus continuity between the Testaments when it comes to glory. What stands out in the New Testament is the uniqueness of Christ's glory, as Hebrews make clear: "He is the radiance of the glory of God and the exact imprint of his nature, and he upholds the universe by the word of his power" (1:3).

Glory is not an attribute of God, like his omnipotence. Rather glory, to follow a suggestion of Christopher Morgan, is a descriptor that summarizes the attributes of God.[41] As we shall see in a subsequent chapter, the astonishing thing is that the glorious God wills to share his glory with us. More than that. God will make us into glorious beings, albeit in a way that our creatureliness remains. We are privileged creatures with a glorious future.

40. Ramm, *Them He Glorified*, 21.
41. Morgan, "Toward a Theology of the Glory of God," 157.

2

The Glorious Divine Project

The university where I teach and whose divinity school I lead is implementing a ten-year plan. There are twelve big goals and 120 sub-goals. In contrast, imagine an institution with no plan. Bankruptcy, among other problems, would be just around the corner. Or think of a country without a defense policy. Invasion may be imminent.

Imagine now a universe without a plan. Some believe that there is no plan—the universe is purposeless. Atheist Lawrence Krauss is a case in point. He argues:

> Imagining living in a universe without purpose may prepare us to better face reality head on. I cannot see that this is such a bad thing. Living in a strange and remarkable universe that is the way it is, independent of our desires and hopes, is far more satisfying for me than living in a fairy-tale universe invented to justify our existence.[1]

1. Lawrence M. Krauss, "A Universe without Purpose," *Los Angeles Times*, April 1, 2012, https://www.latimes.com/. Krauss argues also that "the illusion of purpose and design is perhaps the most pervasive illusion about nature that science has to confront on a daily basis. Everywhere we look, it appears that the world was designed so that we

According to Krauss, we are the products of blind evolution. And yet some secularists argue that we biological organisms have evolved to be purpose driven. Therefore, even on their supposition, at least one corner of the universe is full of purpose. Strange!

The Bible believer knows otherwise. It is not strange that creatures like us, made in the image of a purposeful Creator God, should be purpose driven. But what is that purpose? If there is a divine plan, what is it and how do we fit in?

God's Plan

The God who is there is not silent, as Hebrews 1:1–2 makes clear: "Long ago, at many times and in many ways, God spoke to our fathers by the prophets, but in these last days he has spoken to us by his Son, whom he appointed the heir of all things, through whom also he created the world." There is a revelation from God. The Scriptures are the normative crystallization of that revelation (2 Tim. 3:14–17). The great sixteenth-century Reformer John Calvin was so right to compare Scripture to glasses. He wrote:

> Just as old or bleary-eyed men and those with weak vision, if you thrust before them a most beautiful volume, even if they recognize it to be some sort of writing, yet can scarcely construe two words, but with the aid of spectacles will begin to read distinctly; so Scripture, gathering up the otherwise confused knowledge of God in our minds, having dispersed our dullness, clearly shows us the true God.[2]

The pages of Scripture bring God and his purposes into focus.

could flourish." What a concession, and how strange! The simplest explanation for this phenomenon is that nature has design and purpose.

2. John Calvin, *Institutes of the Christian Religion*, ed. John T. McNeill, trans. Ford Lewis Battles (Philadelphia: Westminster, 1960), 1.6.1.

What then do we see there in the Scriptures? We see the story of the loving God, who not only creates and judges but also saves. J. I Packer sums up the Bible's story in this striking way:

> The first thing we find is that this book is not primarily about man at all. Its subject is God. He (if the phrase be allowed) is the chief actor in the drama, the hero of the story. The Bible proves on inspection to be a factual survey of his work in the world, past, present, and to come, with explanatory comment from prophets, psalmists, wise men and apostles. Its main theme is not human salvation, but the work of God vindicating His purposes and glorifying himself in a sinful and disordered cosmos by establishing His kingdom and exalting His Son, by creating a people to worship and serve Him, and ultimately by dismantling and reassembling this order of things, so rooting sin out of His world entirely.[3]

Packer rightly refers to the works of God and the words of God. Without the "explanatory comments" Packer mentions, the works of God might not be seen as such. How the apostle Paul writes of the cross is a prime example of the need for both work and word. He reminds the Corinthians that "Christ died" but adds "for our sins" (1 Cor. 15:3). Without the explanatory comment, we are left we just another first-century Roman crucifixion story, of which there were thousands.[4] As George Ladd argues, "The historical events are revelatory only when they are accompanied by the revelatory word."[5]

---

3. J. I. Packer, *The Plan of God*, https://www.the-highway.com/, accessed March 28, 2019.

4. On the practice of crucifixion in the Roman world, see Martin Hengel, *Crucifixion* (Philadelphia: Fortress, 1977).

5. George E. Ladd, "The Saving Acts of God," in *Basics of the Faith: An Evangelical Introduction to Christian Doctrine*, ed. Carl F. H. Henry (Bellingham, WA: Lexham, 2019), 27.

Packer, like many others, views Scripture in terms of a drama. Surprisingly, however, literature scholars maintain that in the Scriptures we see not so much a drama but a comedy. Leland Ryken writes, "It is a commonplace of literary criticism that comedy rather than tragedy is the dominant narrative form of the Bible and that Christian Gospel."[6] Now that will take some explaining.

When we think of comedy, we think of stand-ups in a theater, or of a TV show like *The Big Bang Theory*, or of a film like *Guardians of the Galaxy*, which mixes science fiction and comedy. However, from a literary perspective a comedy is literature that has a particular plot shape with a happy ending. Leland Ryken writes: "The overall shape of the biblical story is that of a U-shaped comic plot. The story begins with the creation of a perfect world. It descends into the tragedy of fallen human history. It ends with a new world of total happiness and victory over evil."[7] Although some prefer to use the category of drama to characterize Scripture, comedy is more accurate because it observes the *U* shape of the biblical storyline, according to Ryken.

How right, though, is Ryken to argue that both the Bible and the Christian gospel have a *U* shape?

The Bible's Plotline

The *U* shape of the biblical narrative is quite transparent. The plotline begins with the harmony of Genesis 1–2. The man and the woman are in harmony with God, whose image they bear. They are at home in their environment and in relation to each other. They have fellowship with God and the task of control-

6. Leland Ryken, *A Complete Handbook of Literary Forms in the Bible* (Wheaton, IL: Crossway, 2014), 46.
7. Ryken, *Literary Forms in the Bible*, 46–47.

ling and caring for the garden. That's what the "dominion" of Genesis 1:26 looks like. Their freedom is expansive. They may eat of the fruit of all the trees except one. Chapter 2 ends with the man and the woman described as one flesh, naked and unashamed (vv. 24–25).

Genesis 3, however, relates the story of a catastrophic reversal. The tempter enters the garden zone from the outside. No explanation is offered as to the origin of such a creature. What is clear is that it is an intruder. The serpent soon questions the word of God—"Did God actually say . . . ?"—and, with it, the character of God (Gen. 3:1, 5). The serpent's insinuation is that God is really a withholder of what is desirable. The serpent succeeds, and the primal pair fall into relational disarray. Instead of fellowship with their Creator, they attempt to escape from his presence (Gen. 3:8). Judgment is swift upon the serpent seducer (the devil), the man, and the woman (Gen. 3:14–19).

Intriguingly, in early rabbinic thought, it was argued that Adam lost his glory by his sin in the garden, but the Messiah would restore it. For example, Genesis Rabbah 11 states:

> Adam's glory did not abide the night with him. What is the proof? But Adam passeth not the night in glory (Ps. XLIX, 13). The Rabbis maintain: His glory abode with him, but at the termination of the Sabbath He deprived him of his splendor and expelled him from the Garden of Eden, as it is written, Thou changest his countenance, and sendest him away (Job XIV, 20).[8]

That loss of glory may be reflected in Romans 3:23. Robert Mounce comments on Romans 3:23, "for all have sinned and fall short of the glory of God," in the following illuminating way:

---

8. Quoted in Andrei A. Orlov, "Vested with Adam's Glory: Moses as the Luminous Counterpart of Adam in the Dead Sea Scrolls and in the Macarian Homilies," https://www.marquette.edu/, accessed December 4, 2019.

In Jewish thought humans lost their share in this glory when they broke their relationship to God, but that relationship is to be restored in the age to come. The original intention was that people reflect the glory of God (cf. Gen 1:26). By eating of the tree of the knowledge of good and evil, Adam and Eve sacrificed their relationship to God and determined the essential nature of everyone born into the human race (Gen 3). The redemption provided by Christ enables us to be brought back into a personal relationship with God. Apart from the work of Christ we are unable to effect that restoration.[9]

In rabbinic thought, glory was one of six things Adam lost. The other five were his immortality, his height, the fruit of the earth, the fruit of the trees, and the light of the luminaries in the sky, which became dimmer.[10] Adam and Eve were exiled from Eden and, more importantly, from the presence of God.

From Genesis 3 to Revelation 20, we read of the history of sin and its disastrous consequences, but also of the divine response in saving and judging. The relationship between God and us is fractured (judgment), as are the relationships between the sexes (conflict), our relation to ourselves (shame), and our relation to the environment (thorns and thistles). We are in exile. Life is now lived outside of Eden. The presence of the cherubim with their flaming swords shows that return is no longer possible (Gen. 3:24). Disharmony has replaced harmony. And yet there is hope, for with the judgment comes a promise. A divine intervention will take place, and the enemy of both God and his images will be defeated. The promise of a decisive divine act to come is found in

9. Robert H. Mounce, *Romans*, The New American Commentary (Nashville: Broadman & Holman, 1995), 115.

10. *Midrash Rabbah*, trans. H. Freedman (London: Soncino, 1939), https://archive.org/, accessed June 27, 2019.

Genesis 3:15, in what is known as the *protevangelium* (the first gospel):

> I will put enmity between you and the woman,
>> and between your offspring and her offspring;
> he shall bruise your head,
>> and you shall bruise his heel.

The gospel is the news about that intervention and that restoration of glory.

One way to look at the Bible's story is to see it as, in the main, the story of four sons. Adam, the son of God was tempted in a paradise garden and failed (Gen. 3). Israel, the corporate son of God (Ex. 4:22), was tempted in a wilderness (Ps. 95) and then in a land of promise, a new Eden (Ps. 106), and also failed. However, God sent his own Son to be all that Adam and Israel should have been. This Son of God lived by every word that proceeded out of the mouth of God (cf. Deut. 8:3 and Matt. 4:3–4). He too was tempted but did not fail (Matt. 4:1–11). He stayed true to his messianic mission. In so doing, Jesus truly proved to be the Savior of the world as even the Samaritans acknowledged (John 4:42). Though "the wages of sin is death" (Rom. 6:23), Christ died the death we should die because of our sin (Rom. 5:6–8), and from that death forgiveness flows (Col. 1:13–14). Furthermore, God sent forth his Son so that we might receive adoption as sons and, by the Spirit, call God "Father" (Gal. 4:4–7).[11] A Savior indeed!

Moreover, the cross means the defeat of the serpent. Oscar Cullmann captured the import of that defeat in his well-known analogy.[12] He compared the victory of the cross over evil to

---

11. The Pauline notion of sonship includes both males and females (cf. Gal. 3:27–29 and 4:4–7).

12. Oscar Cullmann, *Christ and Time: The Primitive Christian Conception of Time and History*, trans. Floyd F. Filson (Philadelphia: Westminster, 1964), 84.

the D-Day of World War II, which took place in June 1944. The landing at Normandy was the decisive turning point in the European war. The Nazis were soon in retreat, losing more and more territory. However, they were not finally defeated until May 1945. That final victory is celebrated as V-E Day (Victory in Europe). Even though the decisive victory had been won on D-Day, it would not be consummated until V-E Day.

The writer to the Hebrews captures the significance of the incarnation and the cross: "Since therefore the children share in flesh and blood, he himself [Jesus] likewise partook of the same things, that through death [D-Day, as it were] he might destroy the one who has the power of death, that is, the devil, and deliver all those who through fear of death were subject to lifelong slavery" (Heb. 2:14). However, the devil can still cause menace, while posing as the angel of light, through false teachers (2 Cor. 11:12–15), or resembling a roaring lion through persecution (1 Pet. 5:8). The final victory (V-E Day, as it were) over the devil and his minions remains future, as Revelation 20 shows.

The apostle Paul saw deeply into the import of the divine intervention in these magnificent words:

> But when the fullness of time had come, God sent forth his Son, born of woman, born under the law, to redeem those who were under the law, so that we might receive adoption as sons. And because you are sons, God has sent the Spirit of his Son into our hearts, crying, "Abba! Father!" So you are no longer a slave, but a son, and if a son, then an heir through God. (Gal. 4:4–7)

This excerpt from Galatians is set within a wider argument in which Paul goes all the way back to Abraham and the promises made to him (Gen. 12:1–3).

A key part of Paul's argument is that the nations would be blessed through the foundational promise of Genesis 12 (Gal. 3:7–8). The essential element is faith like Abraham's faith (Gal. 3:9), which trusts the promise of God. Through this faith, both Jew and Gentile receive the promised Holy Spirit (Gal. 3:14). Those who so believe are Abraham's children. However, those children are enslaved by sin and need a deliverer. Thus Christ entered the scene "when the fullness of time had come" (Gal. 4:4).

John Stott rightly comments that the sending of the Son gives us the status of sons through adoption, and the sending of the Spirit of the Son gives us the experience of filial intimacy as we take "Abba" on our lips.[13] Similarly, Paul writes in other places of an inheritance awaiting the children of God (e.g., Rom. 8:12–17). That inheritance is one of the defining characteristics of the glory to come, as the apostle Peter also knew (1 Pet. 1:3–6). Peter describes his readers in these stunning terms: "Though you have not seen him, you love him. Though you do not now see him, you believe in him and rejoice with joy that is inexpressible and filled with glory, obtaining the outcome of your faith, the salvation of your souls" (1 Pet. 1:8–9).

In Paul's letter to the Philippian Christians, the *U* shape of comedy is especially on display as the apostle describes the journey of the Son:

> Have this mind among yourselves, which is yours in Christ Jesus, who, though he was in the form of God, did not count equality with God a thing to be grasped, but emptied himself, by taking the form of a servant, being born in the likeness of men. And being found in human form, he humbled himself by becoming obedient to the point of

---

13. John R. W. Stott, *The Message of Galatians: Only One Way*, The Bible Speaks Today (Downers Grove, IL: InterVarsity Press, 1986), 107.

death, even death on a cross. Therefore God has highly
exalted him and bestowed on him the name that is above
every name, so that at the name of Jesus every knee should
bow, in heaven and on earth and under the earth, and every
tongue confess that Jesus Christ is Lord, to the glory of God
the Father. (2:5–11)

The journey starts in eternity.[14] Jesus is the divine Son who
leaves the state of glory (2:6) and enters the state of humiliation (2:7–8), before returning to the state of glory (2:9–11).
The Son's journey in "spatial" terms is a movement down and
then up again: descent then ascent. The turning point in Philippians 2:5–11 is the cross: "And being found in human form, he
humbled himself by becoming obedient to the point of death,
even death on a cross" (v. 8).

Paul's point to the Philippians is that they ought to be other-
person centered, just like Jesus. They need the humble mind of
Christ because they are pursuing self-interest rather than giving attention to the needs of others. The apostle writes: "Do
nothing from selfish ambition or conceit, but in humility count
others more significant than yourselves. Let each of you look
not only to his own interests, but also to the interests of others" (2:3–4). Paul then draws the Philippians' attention to his
delegate Timothy as exemplifying the way of Christ: "I hope in
the Lord Jesus to send Timothy to you soon, so that I too may
be cheered by news of you. For I have no one like him, who will
be genuinely concerned for your welfare. For they all seek their
own interests, not those of Jesus Christ" (2:19–21). Philippians
2:5–11 is high Christology in the service of pastoral counsel.

The *U* shape of the gospel is also found in the narrative
structure of John's Gospel. The gospel begins in eternity at the

---

14. I am unconvinced by the contention that Paul has Adam in view in Phil. 2:6, and
that Paul is contrasting Jesus (humility) and Adam (pride).

summit: "In the beginning was the Word, and the Word was with God, and the Word was God. He was in the beginning with God" (John 1:1–2). However, the Word did not remain in eternity, for we read in verse 14, "The Word became flesh and dwelt among us, and we have seen his glory, glory as of the only Son from the Father, full of grace and truth." The unfolding of the story of the Word become flesh is simple in language but ever so deep in meaning and carefully constructed. When we read through John 1:1–18, we come to know that the Word is actually the Son, and that "glory" is an apt descriptor of him because he embodies the great values of the covenant: "grace and truth" (v. 14). The prologue unfolds yet more about the identity of the Word. The climax of the prologue tells us: "For the law was given through Moses; grace and truth came through Jesus Christ. No one has ever seen God; the only God, who is at the Father's side, he has made him known" (John 1:17–18). The Word, who is the Son, has a human name, "Jesus Christ." The Word, the Son, Jesus Christ has entered the sphere of fallenness (the state of humiliation) with a mission to make the Father known and to glorify his Father (John 17:4).

So, although he is the incarnate Son, the Word become flesh, he gets tired and he gets thirsty (John 4:6–7). He reaches his lowest point, his most degrading condition, his nadir on the cross, where in his role as the Lamb of God he bears away the sins of the world (John 1:29). Yet, paradoxically, it is also his enthronement (John 12:32). Death does not hold him. He is raised and tells his disciples of his return to the Father (John 20:17). Importantly for our purposes, Jesus describes this journey in glory categories. In the garden he prays, shortly before his death, "And now, Father, glorify me in your own presence with the glory that I had with you before the world existed"

(John 17:5). Once again, we see the comedic pattern of movement: from up to down, then up again.

This pattern is also found in Hebrews 1–2. The Son of God is "the radiance of the glory of God and the exact imprint of his nature, and he upholds the universe by the word of his power" (1:3). The Son is indeed the object of angelic worship (1:5–6).[15] This is one of a number of New Testament passages that affirm the deity of Christ (e.g., John 1:1–2; Phil. 2:5–6). The Son becomes human, "made lower than the angels," that he might taste death for wayward creatures such as us. That death results in Jesus's being crowned with glory and honor (Heb. 2:9). The third explicit reference to glory in Hebrews brings Christology, anthropology, soteriology, and eschatology together: "For it was fitting that he, for whom and by whom all things exist, in bringing [soteriology] many sons [anthropology] to glory [eschatology], should make the founder of their salvation [Christology] perfect through suffering" (Heb. 2:10).

But why? What is the divine intention?

The Purpose of It All

The God of the Bible pursues his own glory, as the prophet Isaiah makes plain:

> For my own sake, for my own sake, I do it,
> for how should my name be profaned?
> My glory I will not give to another. (Isa. 48:11)

15. That Jesus is the object of both human and angelic worship is strong proof that the New Testament writers did not have a low Christology. A low Christology that views Jesus as merely human without remainder would make the worship of him nothing less than idolatry, and would render passages such as Rev. 5:6–14 unfathomable. See Richard Bauckham, *The Theology of the Book of Revelation* (Cambridge, UK: Cambridge University Press, 2016), 58–63. For a high Christology, see Stephen J. Wellum, *God the Son Incarnate: The Doctrine of Christ* (Wheaton, IL: Crossway, 2016), and Wellum., *The Person of Christ: An Introduction* (Wheaton, IL: Crossway, 2020).

In expounding Paul's letter to the Ephesians, Christopher Morgan helpfully unfolds the meaning of the divine pursuit:

> First, God acts in order to receive worship and praise from his creation, especially his people (1:6, 12, 14). Second, God acts to display himself throughout creation. He displays his love, mercy, grace, kindness, creative work, and wisdom (2:4–10; 3:8–10). As he displays himself, he communicates his greatness and fullness and thereby glorifies himself.[16]

Unsurprisingly, the divine pursuit ought to shape the role of humankind. The Westminster Shorter Catechism puts it this way: "Man's chief end is to glorify God and enjoy him forever."[17] John Piper has put an original twist on this centuries-old claim: "The chief end of man is to glorify God BY enjoying him forever."[18] This is a controversial claim, whether in the original or the revised version. Some might think that such a pursuit betrays a kind of celestial narcissism. Imagine a new president who announces at his inauguration that his agenda is to glorify himself. J. I. Packer is right to contend: "Now this is a truth which at first we find hard to receive. Our immediate reaction to it is an uncomfortable feeling that such an idea is unworthy of God: that self-concern of any sort is really incompatible with moral perfection, and in particular with God's nature as love."[19]

One answer is that God is God and we are not. What would be a morally wrong pursuit for a creature is not so for the Creator. Packer embraces this answer when he writes:

16. Christopher W. Morgan, "The Church and God's Glory," in *The Community of Jesus: A Theology of the Church*, ed. Kendall H. Easley and Christopher W. Morgan (Nashville: B&H, 2013), 215.

17. Westminster Shorter Catechism, Q. 1, Westminster Shorter Catechism Project, http://www.shortercatechism.com/, accessed March 28, 2019.

18. John Piper, *Desiring God: Meditations of a Christian Hedonist* (Portland, OR: Multnomah, 1986), 14, 19, original emphasis.

19. Packer, *Plan of God*.

God's end in all His acts is ultimately Himself. There is nothing morally dubious about this; if we allow that man can have no higher end than the glory of God, how can we say anything different about God Himself? The idea that it is somehow unworthy to represent God as aiming at His own glory in all that He does seems to reflect a failure to remember that God and man are not on the same level; and to show lack of realization that, whereas a man who makes his own well-being his ultimate end does so at the expense of his fellow-creatures, God has determined to glorify Himself by blessing His creatures.[20]

This answer rightly recognizes the ontological and qualitative difference between the Creator and the creature.

Still another answer is that God is triune. The Father glorifies the Son, the Son glorifies the Father, and the Holy Spirit glorifies both the Father and the Son. In John's Gospel, in dialogue with his disciples, Jesus states, with oblique reference to himself, "Now is the Son of Man glorified [the cross is in view as though it has already happened], and God is glorified in him. If God is glorified in him, God will also glorify him in himself, and glorify him at once" (John 13:31–32). Jesus's prayer in the garden of Gethsemane is also germane at this point. He sums up his earthly ministry in these terms addressed to the Father: "I glorified you on earth" (John 17:3). With regard to the ministry of the Holy Spirit, Jesus is direct: "He will glorify me" (John 16:14). Glorifying the other is a divine activity within the Godhead. Thus, when creatures are called on to glorify their Maker, they are being commanded to be like their God.

The glorious God of biblical revelation is willing to share his glory, as Romans 8:28–30 shows:

20. Packer, *Plan of God*.

And we know that for those who love God all things work together for good, for those who are called according to his purpose. For those whom he foreknew he also predestined to be conformed to the image of his Son, in order that he might be the firstborn among many brothers. And those whom he predestined he also called, and those whom he called he also justified, and those whom he justified he also glorified.

The God who pursues his own glory pursues ours as well. What grace!

The Golden Chain of Redemption

Romans 8:30 is especially illuminating with regard to the divine answer to the catastrophic defection of humankind. The elements that Paul names form the "golden chain" of redemption: predestination, calling, justification, and glorification. The phrase "golden chain" goes back to the great Anglican Puritan William Perkins, of the sixteenth century.[21] He understood that the elect individual is the subject of every element making up the chain.

However, contemporary Arminians read this text differently. They argue that foreknowledge is the key, and the church is in view, not individuals.[22] God foreknows a class of human beings who will become believers. These believers are the church. This class *qua* class is predestined to be the sphere of justification and glorification. The theological issue is whether foreknowledge is contingent upon fore-determination

21. William Perkins published a book in 1592 titled *A Golden Chain or the Description of Salvation*. I have shortened the lengthy title. The full title, as translated from the Latin, is *A golden Chaine, or The Description of Theologie, containing the order of the causes of Salvation and Damnation, according to Gods word*.
22. For example, see William G. McDonald, "The Biblical Doctrine of Election," in *A Case for Arminianism: The Grace of God, The Will of Man*, ed. Clark H. Pinnock (Grand Rapids, MI: Zondervan, 1989), 226.

or predestination is contingent upon foreknowledge of repentance and faith.[23]

What can be said of this controversial golden chain? This is a text that allows conjunctive theology: *both–and* rather than *either–or*. Bruce Demarest gets it right in his discussion of Romans 8:29–30. He argues: "The circle of salvation is both corporate and individual."[24] And again, he contends: "If we talk of the election of a class, it must be as the sum of elect individuals."[25] The staggering truth to observe is that God will glorify those whom he justifies. This glory sharing is well summed up by Morgan when he writes, "The idea of the uniquely glorious God sharing his glory with his people would appear bizarre, except for the fact that it is such a prominent theme. The breadth of the New Testament teaching on this is astounding."[26] Morgan is right, and Romans 8:30 is only one such text.

The divine project broadly considered is nothing less than the restoration of true worship throughout creation. This is the *eternal* gospel. John the apostle declares:

23. I myself think that divine foreknowledge is informed by divine determination. However, I have respected colleagues who think otherwise. My difficulty with the Arminian position is manyfold. For a start, it seems to me that any account of human freedom needs to start with God, which is where the Bible itself starts (Gen.1:1). By that I mean that any account of human freedom needs to be related to the sovereignty of God—after all, in Gen. 1, God comes before us as the great King who rules by his word—and not start with human freedom and then ask how God's sovereignty fits with it. More specifically, there are texts of Scripture that seem to clearly refer to the divine choice of individuals and not a class (e.g., Acts 13:48). Lastly, the reality of total depravity makes divine election a necessity. The Arminian doctrine posits a universal prevenient grace, which puts every fallen person into a position of being able to respond freely to the gospel by counteracting total depravity. However, the biblical evidence points to the inability of sinners to respond to the gospel unless God acts sovereignly toward them. It is Jesus's sheep who are his own, and it is they who listen to his voice—namely, the elect (John 10:14–16, 25–30). For further discussion of this controversial subject, see Andrew Naselli's forthcoming book on election and reprobation in this series.

24. Bruce Demarest, *The Cross and Salvation: The Doctrine of Salvation* (Wheaton, IL: Crossway, 1997), 129.

25. Demarest, *The Cross and Salvation*, 135.

26. Christopher W. Morgan, "Toward a Theology of the Glory of God," in *The Glory of God*, ed. Christopher W. Morgan and Robert A. Peterson (Wheaton, IL: Crossway, 2010), 170.

> Then I saw another angel flying directly overhead, with an eternal gospel to proclaim to those who dwell on earth, to every nation and tribe and language and people. And he said with a loud voice, "Fear God and give him glory, because the hour of his judgment has come, and worship him who made heaven and earth, the sea and the springs of water." (Rev. 14:6–7)

Narrowly considered in relation to us, then, it is nothing less than masterpiece restoration, and such a restoration results in our glorification. Morna Hooker writes perceptively: "It is Christ who is the basis of hope, and the object of hope is glory. In Romans, Paul tells the story of how Adam lost God's glory (1:23; 3:23) and how believers now hope for that glory's restoration (5:12; 8:18, 30)."[27]

Haley Goranson Jacob offers an intriguing suggestion as to how Romans 8:30, with its glorification motif, is to be understood. This Pauline text, according to her, is not about salvation but vocation. The golden chain of redemption is really the golden chain of vocation. In a close reading of Paul's letter to the Romans, she sees a narrative of glory. In this narrative what was lost in Adam is regained in Christ, and through union with him believers participate in his kingly rule. For them, "to be glorified is to experience a transformation of status—to be exalted to a new status, one of honor associated with a representative reign over creation, crowned with glory as Adam was meant to be and as the Messiah now is."[28] Jacob argues that the Greek underlying the English translation "glorified" (aorist aspect) is to be understood as meaning that glorification has already taken place.[29] Believers participate in Christ's rule now.

---

27. Morna D. Hooker, "Colossians," in *Eerdmans Commentary on the Bible*, ed. James D. G. Dunn and John W. Rogerson (Grand Rapids, MI: Eerdmans, 2003), 1407.

28. Haley Goranson Jacob, *Conformed to the Image of His Son: Reconsidering Paul's Theology of Glory in Romans* (Downers Grove, IL: IVP Academic, 2018), 121.

29. Jacob, *Conformed to the Image*, 237.

However, Jacob also recognizes that Romans 8:17 claims that "the glory of believers is yet to come."[30] Paul writes there, "And if children, then heirs—heirs of God and fellow heirs with Christ, provided we suffer with him in order that we may also be glorified with him." Jacob makes sense of Romans 8:17 (future) and Romans 8:30 (now) when Paul is seen as working with the concept of "now but not yet" (inaugurated eschatology). I am persuaded that she is right to contend that glorification has two stages in Paul's thought. As she says: "On the basis of believers' union with Christ, glorification is a present reality, at least in part. . . . When believers' bodies are resurrected to share in the glory of Christ, as in Philippians 3:21, then they will do so fully."[31] This raises a question: Do you agree with Jacob's proposal that it refers to vocation, not salvation? Could it be both?

Conclusion

The universe is not a capricious place where chance rules. Humankind is no cosmic accident. The glorious God has made humankind in the divine image, but that image is now sadly defaced. To be fully in the image of God is to be a glorified being. How could it not be since that image, more precisely put, is the image of Christ. The glory Adam lost, Christ as the new Adam regains for us. That means we share in the identity and status of corulers with Christ. That God pursues his own glory should not surprise us. God is God, and we are not. Yet the glorious God is the glory-sharing God. Extraordinary! This is not a case of celestial self-absorption. The doctrine of the Trinity alerts

30. Jacob, *Conformed to the Image*, 233.
31. Jacob, *Conformed to the Image*, 237. It has been said that people are largely right in what they affirm and wrong in what they deny. Jacob makes a good case for the vocational aspect of glorification, but does that preclude the soteriological? Why not both–and? One could argue that only a glorified being can carry out the Christlike rule for which she argues.

us to the fact that the glorious God is triune and that mutual glorifying is characteristic of the Trinity *ad intra* (on the inside). Our glorifying God is to act in a Godlike way. The question, though, is Just what does our glorification involve? What does the pathway to glorification look like? To this we next turn.

3

The Pathway to Glory

Is the idea of glorification an opiate for the masses? Karl Marx would have thought so. He argued that religion leads the believer to focus on the prospect of the world to come and to neglect this one. He famously wrote: "Religion is the sigh of the oppressed creature, the heart of a heartless world, and the soul of soulless conditions. It is the *opium* of the people."[1] He described heaven as a fantasy.[2] This is the proverbial "pie-in-the-sky-when-you-die" mentality, to borrow a line from a song written by Joe Hill in 1911. Hill was an activist for organized labor. His song parodies the well-known Christian hymn "In the Sweet By-and-By." However, as we shall see, the biblical testimony is that the process of glorification has already begun in this life. Moreover, as we shall also see, the prospect of glory provides motivation to live a godly life in the here and now. The prospect of the world to come should lead believers to service in this one. Furthermore, glorification as a process and a prospect

1. Karl Marx, introduction to "A Contribution to the Critique of Hegel's Philosophy of Right," Marxist Internet Archive, https://www.marxists.org/, accessed November 8, 2019.
2. Marx, introduction.

is a work of the triune God. It is a gospel benefit. We begin with the role of the Father.

The Role of the Father

Earliest Christianity faced persecution from the Jewish authorities in Jerusalem as the story of the first martyr, Stephen, shows. In his dramatic speech before the Jewish authorities, Stephen described God in these terms: "Brothers and fathers, hear me. The God of glory appeared to our father Abraham when he was in Mesopotamia, before he lived in Haran" (Acts 7:2). The reaction to the speech was violent: "Now when they [the Jewish authorities] heard these things they were enraged, and they ground their teeth at him"(Acts 7:54). Stephen was then stoned to death (Acts 7:59). But before he was killed for the faith, God granted him a vision. Stephen had spoken of the God of glory appearing to Abraham. Now he saw for himself, in his final moments, the glory of this same God : "But he, full of the Holy Spirit, gazed into heaven and saw the glory of God, and Jesus standing at the right hand of God"(Acts 7:55). It is no surprise, then, that the apostle Paul likewise described God the Father in similar terms. He prayed for the Ephesians "that the God of our Lord Jesus Christ, the Father of glory, may give you the Spirit of wisdom and of revelation in the knowledge of him" (Eph. 1:17).[3] As we saw in a previous chapter, God is indeed glorious.

The Gospel of John clearly asserts the oneness of God and yet affirms distinctions within the Godhead (John 1:1–2; 10:30). One of those distinctions is featured in Jesus's famous prayer in the upper room.[4] Jesus prayed, "And now, Father,

---

3. Paul consistently uses the descriptor "God" of the Father (e.g., 1 Cor. 12:4–7; Eph. 1:3).

4. For a deep discussion of the triune oneness and distinctions within the Godhead, see Scott R. Swain's work in this series, *The Trinity: An Introduction* (Wheaton, IL: Crossway, 2020).

glorify me in your own presence with the glory that I had with you before the world existed" (John 17:5). Richard Bauckham comments: "I doubt that this refers mainly to honor, though honor is entailed. This glory is a glory that can be seen (17:24). It is the manifest splendor, the glory of God that no one can see and live, the unveiled radiance of 'who God is.'"[5] This claim is striking because it asserts so clearly the preexistence of the Son and that the Son has given up splendor in becoming incarnate, which he prays will be restored.

Christ's giving up his glory has led to a plethora of theories as to what such an emptying might have entailed, especially when Paul's letter to the Philippians is brought into the conversation. In that letter, Paul famously challenges the Philippian Christians, "Have this mind among yourselves, which is yours in Christ Jesus, who, though he was in the form of God, did not count equality with God a thing to be grasped, but emptied himself, by taking the form of a servant, being born in the likeness of men" (Phil. 2:5–7).

Did the Son give up his omnipotence, his omnipresence, and his omniscience? What we can safely say is that he gave up his splendor as the Son *by* becoming incarnate. Such was his humility.[6] Paul captures that humility in a different way in his second letter to the Corinthians: "For you know the grace of our Lord Jesus Christ, that though he was rich, yet for your sake he became poor, so that you by his poverty might become rich" (2 Cor. 8:9). Murray J. Harris comments:

5. Richard Bauckham, *Gospel of Glory: Major Themes in Johannine Theology* (Grand Rapids, MI: Baker Academic, 2015), 59–60.

6. Theories that make much of the humility of the Son in the incarnation are called kenotic theories, from the Greek verb *ekenōsen* ("he emptied"), used by Paul in Phil. 2:7. The most extreme theory is that of Thomas J. J. Altizer, who argued that the Son gave up being God and was only a man when he died on the cross. God is therefore no more. This view is bizarre! See "Interview with Thomas J. J. Altizer," by Lissa McCullough, *Journal for Cultural and Religious Theory* 12, no. 3 (2013): 169–85, https://jcrt.org/, accessed May 7, 2020.

In this verse, then, Paul is reminding the Corinthians how gracious the Lord Jesus Christ was, for although (ὤν) he was rich beyond telling in the glory of his preexistent life in heaven, he became desperately poor in comparison with that richness, by assuming the relative poverty of his whole life on earth, a poverty that paradoxically brought believers spiritual enrichment.[7]

This Pauline text is also important because it points to our rich destiny. That enrichment, as Mark Seifrid argues, comprises a myriad of blessings, including glory: "Correspondingly, the riches that Christ communicates consist in righteousness, life, glory, and comfort—in other words, the gift of salvation itself."[8]

According to Paul, we are called by God the Father to a wonderful prospect: the kingdom and glory. Paul writes to the Thessalonians: "You know how, like a father with his children, we exhorted each one of you and encouraged you and charged you to walk in a manner worthy of God, who calls you into his own kingdom and glory" (1 Thess. 2:11–12). This prospect should have here-and-now behavioral consequences. We are to reflect the character of God. An operational theology ought to flow from our espoused theology. If we espouse this glorious kingdom prospect, then there is a lifestyle or, to use the Pauline idiom, "a walk" that goes with it.

The Role of the Son

Jesus is the Lord of glory. Paul uses this phrase in 1 Corinthians 2:8: "None of the rulers of this age understood this, for if they

---

7. Murray J. Harris, *The Second Epistle to the Corinthians: A Commentary on the Greek Text*, The New International Greek Testament Commentary (Grand Rapids, MI: Eerdmans; Milton Keynes, UK: Paternoster, 2005), 580.

8. Mark A. Seifrid, *The Second Letter to the Corinthians*, The Pillar New Testament Commentary (Grand Rapids, MI: Eerdmans; Cambridge, UK: Apollos, 2014), 330.

had, they would not have crucified the Lord of glory." This title has been variously interpreted. Augustine thought it referred to Jesus dispensing glory. Still others translate it as "glorious Lord." James also uses the phrase: "My brothers, show no partiality as you hold the faith in our Lord Jesus Christ, the Lord of glory" (James 2:1). Peter Davids contends, "To speak of Christ as glorious is to speak of his reputation, fame, or honor."[9] J. A. Motyer adds further insight: "Glory, then, is 'shorthand' for the personal presence of the Lord in all his goodness and in the fullness of his revealed character. The Lord Jesus Christ is God's Glory: God himself come among us in all his goodness and in the full revelation of his person."[10]

The Father shares his glory with the Son, and the Son shares his glory with us. In his Upper Room Discourse, Jesus prays to the Father on behalf of his disciples, "The glory that you have given me I have given to them, that they may be one even as we are one" (John 17:22). Gerald L. Borchert rightly observes: "The disciples' glory must be understood as derivative of the glory of the Godhead. This glory is not something innate in them."[11] It is a mediated glory. Jesus goes on to pray: "Father, I desire that they also, whom you have given me, may be with me where I am, to see my glory that you have given me because you loved me before the foundation of the world" (John 17:24). Indeed, Jesus sees his future return in glory terms with a view to judging all the nations: "When the Son of Man comes in his glory, and all the angels with him, then he will sit on his glorious throne" (Matt. 25:31). The early church recognized the importance of this teaching by making it part of the confession

9. Peter H. Davids, *The Epistle of James: A Commentary on the Greek Text*, The New International Greek Testament Commentary (Grand Rapids, MI: Eerdmans, 1982), 107.
10. J. A. Motyer, *The Message of James: The Tests of Faith*, The Bible Speaks Today (Leicester: Inter-Varsity Press, 1985), 82–86.
11. Gerald L. Borchert, *John 12–21*, The New American Commentary (Nashville: Broadman & Holman, 2002), 207.

of faith as found in the Nicene-Constantinopolitan Creed of AD 381:

> He will come again in glory
> to judge the living and the dead
> and his kingdom will have no end.[12]

The end-time picture is as Craig Blomberg rightly describes: "The picture is one of grandeur, majesty, authority, and judgment."[13]

How then does the risen Christ share his glory with his followers?

The Role of the Holy Spirit

As we have seen, the Father is the Father of glory, and Jesus is the Lord of glory. Unsurprisingly, we also find in the New Testament that the Holy Spirit is the Spirit of glory. Peter has persecuted Christians in mind when he writes: "If you are insulted for the name of Christ, you are blessed, because the Spirit of glory and of God rests upon you" (1 Pet. 4:14). The ESV is correct to capitalize "Spirit." Wayne Grudem usefully comments: "*The spirit* ('Spirit,' as in NIV, NASB, TEV, would be better, since it is certainly the Holy Spirit who is the Spirit of God) *of glory and of God rests upon you* indicates an unusual fullness of the presence of the Holy Spirit to bless, to strengthen, and to give a foretaste of heavenly glory."[14] The story of Stephen illustrates the point. In his martyrdom, Stephen, full of the Spirit, saw the divine glory (Acts 7:55).

---

12. "Nicene Creed," Britannica (website), https://www.britannica.com/, accessed October 14, 2019.

13. Craig L. Blomberg, *Matthew: An Exegetical and Theological Exposition of Holy Scripture*, The New American Commentary (Nashville: Broadman & Holman, 1992), 376.

14. Wayne A. Grudem, *1 Peter: An Introduction and Commentary*, Tyndale New Testament Commentaries (Downers Grove, IL: InterVarsity Press, 1988), 186–87, original emphasis.

The role of the Holy Spirit in our glorification is addressed by the apostle Paul in his second letter to the Corinthian church. The passage we need to consider, 2 Corinthians 3:7–18, is a challenging one and commentators debate its meaning at multiple levels. In it, Paul contrasts two ministries.

Paul begins with "the ministry of death" in Moses's time (v. 7). He is referring to Sinai and the giving of the Ten Commandments, written on stone (v. 7). Paul points out that the Israelites could not look on Moses's face because of its glory (v. 7). This "ministry of death" was a "ministry of condemnation" (v. 9). Paul does not elaborate, but he is most probably thinking of their inability to keep the law and their facing divine condemnation for it. Moses veiled his face because the glory was fading (v. 13). Paul makes the point that in his own day, Jews have the same hardened minds as their ancestors. The veil remains over their hearts, as it were, hiding the glory, and only Christ can take the veil away (v. 14).

However, there is another ministry: "the ministry of the Spirit," "the ministry of righteousness" (vv. 8–9). Paul uses an *a fortiori* argument (a "how much more" argument). If a glory was seen in Moses's day, in Christ and the Spirit's day there is a greater glory still (vv. 9–11). This glory is permanent and unfading. The veil is removed (v. 16). Moreover, with the Spirit's ministry come freedom and transformation (v. 17). Paul writes: "And we all, with unveiled face, beholding the glory of the Lord, are being transformed into the same image from one degree of glory to another" (v. 18). Scholars debate whether Paul's language "we all . . . are being transformed [present aspect] . . . from one degree of glory to another" suggest a linear progression (the view of, e.g., Thomas Smail and Colin Kruse) or is simply claiming that the transformation has immediacy and is vivid experientially (the view of, e.g., Mark

Seifrid).[15] I find that Kruse and Smail are more convincing. Since Paul argues that our inner nature can be renewed every day (2 Cor. 4:16), and this is a continuous reality, why not also the transforming work of the Spirit?

But how, exactly, does this transformation come about? Thomas Smail helpfully comments:

> As he [the believer] thus looks to Christ and opens himself to him, the knowledge of Christ that he gains is never simply objective and intellectual knowledge, it is knowledge that begins to change him, so that he begins to reflect that to which he has been exposed, and its likeness begins to be formed in him.[16]

As for "the glory of the Lord" again, Smail is correct to argue, "Glory means here the revealed person, character, work and power of the Lord Jesus Christ."[17] Indeed, Paul goes on to claim that the glory of God is found in the face of Jesus Christ (2 Cor. 4:6).

Clearly, the glorification process begins now, as 2 Corinthians 3:18 shows: it is from glory to glory. And the Spirit of Christ is the transforming agent.

A Trinitarian Work

It is fundamental to Trinitarian theology that each person of the Trinity is involved in every divine act, albeit in distinct but inseparable ways.[18] In terms of the big picture of the plan of

15. Cf. Thomas A. Smail, *Reflected Glory: The Spirit in Christ and Christians* (London: Hodder and Stoughton, 1975), 27–28; Colin G. Kruse, *2 Corinthians: An Introduction and Commentary*, Tyndale New Testament Commentaries (Downers Grove, IL: InterVarsity Press, 1987), 101–2; Seifrid, *Second Letter to the Corinthians*, 186.

16. Smail, *Reflected Glory*, 25–26.

17. Smail, *Reflected Glory*, 26.

18. Augustine captures this axiom of Trinitarian theology in this way: "All the works of the Trinity to the outside are indivisible" (*Omnia opera trinitatis ad extra indivisa sunt*).

salvation, the Father is the architect, the Son its accomplisher, and the Holy Spirit its applier. Paul provides a fine example of Trinitarian thinking with a glory note in his second letter to the Thessalonians:

> But we ought always to give thanks to God for you, brothers beloved by the Lord, because God chose you as the firstfruits to be saved, through sanctification by the Spirit and belief in the truth. To this he called you through our gospel, so that you may obtain the glory of our Lord Jesus Christ. (2 Thess. 2:13–14)

Obtaining the glory of our Lord Jesus Christ is a work of the Trinity: Father, Son, and Holy Spirit. The Father chooses us, the Son loves us, and the Spirit sanctifies us.

Two Paradoxes of Glorification

There are two paradoxes to consider regarding glorification and our experience in following Christ. The first has to do with the outer and the inner. As we have seen, the apostle Paul conceived of glorification as beginning in the here and now: from one degree of glory to the next (2 Cor. 3:18). This is a matter of faith, not sight. I am no longer a young man. To look at me is not to look at a glorious being. Paul knew the truth of the paradox and the Christian's need for encouragement. He wrote to the Corinthians: "So we do not lose heart. Though our outer self [lit. "the outward humanity"] is wasting away, our inner self [lit. "our inward"] is being renewed day by day" (2 Cor. 4:16–18). However, Paul lived in the light of eternity, and so he went on to write: "For this light momentary affliction is preparing for us an eternal weight of glory beyond all comparison, as we look not to the things that are seen but to the things that are unseen. For the things that are seen are transient, but the things that are unseen are eternal" (2 Cor. 4:17–18).

Becket Cook, a Hollywood set designer, experienced a dramatic conversion from gay atheist to devout follower of Christ. He still wrestles with same-sex attraction, but for him the prospect of an eternal weight of glory more than compensates for the desires rightly left unfulfilled. He writes: "These verses [2 Cor. 4:17–18] are always a salve to the soul when I struggle with temptation. (Yes, I still do!) . . . It is hard to fathom the eternal weight of glory, but I know it is infinitely more gratifying than any ephemeral pleasure on this earth."[19]

The second paradox is that even though we can be transformed from one degree of glory to the next, we may also experience great suffering at the very same time. In fact, the path to glory is Christomorphic—that is to say, Christ-shaped. Christ suffered as the Son of Man before entering his glory, and he warned his disciples that suffering would be their experience too. In the upper room, he spoke plainly: "Remember the word that I said to you: 'A servant is not greater than his master.' If they persecuted me, they will also persecute you. If they kept my word, they will also keep yours" (John 15:20). The apostle Peter understood his Master's point: "And after you have suffered a little while, the God of all grace, who has called you to his eternal glory in Christ, will himself restore, confirm, strengthen, and establish you" (1 Pet. 5:10).

The prime example of a believer treading that path is the apostle Paul, and out of all his letters, his second letter to the Corinthians is most revelatory of the personal cost he experienced in following Christ. It is striking that Paul despaired of life itself, such was his depression at one juncture. He wrote:

19. Becket Cook, *A Change of Affection: A Gay Man's Incredible Story of Redemption* (Nashville: Thomas Nelson, 2019), 148.

"For we do not want you to be unaware, brothers, of the affliction we experienced in Asia. For we were so utterly burdened beyond our strength that we despaired of life itself. Indeed, we felt that we had received the sentence of death" (2 Cor. 1:8–9). Even so, as a man of faith, he understood the lesson of such an experience: "But that was to make us rely not on ourselves but on God who raises the dead" (2 Cor. 1:9). Later in the same letter, Paul gives a more granular delineation of what his apostolic sufferings entailed. His aim is to undermine the claim of some who were troubling the Corinthians, teachers who were asserting their superiority over Paul.

> But whatever anyone else dares to boast of—I am speaking as a fool—I also dare to boast of that. Are they Hebrews? So am I. Are they Israelites? So am I. Are they offspring of Abraham? So am I. Are they servants of Christ? I am a better one—I am talking like a madman—with far greater labors, far more imprisonments, with countless beatings, and often near death. Five times I received at the hands of the Jews the forty lashes less one. Three times I was beaten with rods. Once I was stoned. Three times I was shipwrecked; a night and a day I was adrift at sea; on frequent journeys, in danger from rivers, danger from robbers, danger from my own people, danger from Gentiles, danger in the city, danger in the wilderness, danger at sea, danger from false brothers; in toil and hardship, through many a sleepless night, in hunger and thirst, often without food, in cold and exposure. And, apart from other things, there is the daily pressure on me of my anxiety for all the churches. (2 Cor. 11:21–28)

And yet, as we have seen, he could also write in the same letter:

> So we do not lose heart. Though our outer self is wasting away, our inner self is being renewed day by day. For this

light momentary affliction is preparing for us an eternal weight of glory beyond all comparison, as we look not to the things that are seen but to the things that are unseen. (2 Cor. 4:16–18)

Given this second paradox, there is no place for Pollyanna-ism in serious discipleship.[20] Prosperity-gospel teaching looks a lot like Pollyannaism. I recall being told that the King's kids travel first class. Really? John the Baptist was imprisoned and subsequently beheaded (Mark 6:14–29), Jesus died on a cross in a shockingly cruel form of execution (Mark 15:21–39), and Paul wrote of his extreme suffering as an apostle (2 Cor. 12:1–10). And yet, Jesus endured the cross in the light of the joy that lay beyond it (Heb. 12:2). There is an eternal weight of glory ahead, but "ahead" is the key idea. To expect more than the Bible promises is to fall into over-realized eschatology, as though we are in heaven now, which clearly we are not.

Prospect, Process, and Service

The prospect of glory does not leave the believer indolent about the present. Marx was wrong about a robust biblical faith. However, he may have been right about the kind of cultural Christianity he witnessed around him. We are a people in process, as we have seen in Paul's second Corinthian letter. Paul again points the way on this question. In Colossians 3:1–4 he argues:

If then you have been raised with Christ, seek the things that are above, where Christ is, seated at the right hand of God. Set your minds on things that are above, not on things that are on earth. For you have died, and your life is hidden with Christ in God. When Christ who is your life appears, then you also will appear with him in glory.

20. Pollyannaism is an unrealistic optimism in the face of adversity.

Paul places the heavenly reality squarely in front of the Colossians, and the verbs "seek" (v. 1) and "set" (v. 2) are significant. His rationale lies in our union with Christ, for we have died with him in some sense and now live in him (v. 3). The prospect of glory with Christ is the consequent promise (v. 4). All this might suggest that Marx was right.

However, Paul continues the argument with a clothing metaphor. In so doing, he shows that to seek the things above and to set one's mind on things above have consequences for this life. Douglas Moo is right to comment, "Believers 'seek the things above' by deliberately and daily committing ourselves to the values of the heavenly kingdom and living out of those values."[21] But how exactly is this to be done? The old self is to be put off like a garment with its sinful practices (Col. 3:9). Paul gives quite a list of vices (Col. 3:5–9): sexual immorality, impurity, passion, evil desire, covetousness, anger, wrath, malice, slander, and obscene talk. Positively, the Colossians are to put on a new garment of godly virtues (Col. 3:12–14): compassion, kindness, humility, meekness, patience, and, above all, love. Importantly, Paul argues that this putting off and putting on flows from the heavenly dimension and prospect. The key word is "therefore," found in Colossians 3:5: "Put to death therefore [Greek, *oun*] what is earthly in you." The word is used again when Paul turns to the godly virtues in Colossians 3:12: "Put on then [Greek, *oun*], as God's chosen ones, holy and beloved, compassionate hearts, kindness, humility, meekness, and patience." This shows that in Paul's mind there is a logical connection between Colossians 3:1–4 and what follows.

The prospect of glory is no opiate. Marx was wrong.

---

21. Douglas J. Moo, *The Letters to the Colossians and to Philemon*, The Pillar New Testament Commentary (Grand Rapids, MI: Eerdmans, 2008), 246.

Do We Play Any Role in Our Glorification?

Apparently, we are not active in our glorification! Glorification appears to be a divine work and not a cooperative one. Thomas Smail rightly says, "This change [referring to 2 Cor. 3:18] is not something which we do, but always something that is done to us, as we open ourselves in faith to the Lord."[22] Not all agree. David E. Garland argues in his comment on 2 Corinthians 3:18:

> The Spirit is not imposed upon us, and Christians must engage in spiritual disciplines that make the Spirit's work possible in changing our lives at the fundamental level. God's Spirit empowers us to do what we want to do and makes what we want to do to be what is right so that Christlikeness flows from us naturally.[23]

Paul Barnett is of the same mind as Garland when he writes in his discussion of verse 18, "We must take steps to place ourselves under the ministry of the gospel through church membership and also by personal Bible reading and prayer."[24]

However, the idea of glorification needs to be distinguished from two others to do justice to the biblical testimony. Garland and Barnett fail to do this. Glorification needs to be distinguished from progressive sanctification and complete sanctification. Progressive sanctification refers to our progress in becoming like Christ. It is a cooperative reality involving both the agency of the Holy Spirit and our own (cf. Phil. 2:12–13 and 1 Thess. 4:1–8). It seems to me that Garland and Barnett have very helpful insights into progressive sanctification, but I do not believe that 2 Corinthians 3:18 is about that. Complete sancti-

22. Smail, *Reflected* Glory, 28.
23. David E. Garland, *2 Corinthians*, The New American Commentary (Nashville: Broadman and Holman, 1999), 201–2.
24. Paul Barnett, *The Message of 2 Corinthians: Power in Weakness*, The Bible Speaks Today (Leicester: Inter-Varsity Press, 1988), 75.

fication refers to the eschatological prospect of God's making us blameless in his sight. Paul writes, "Now may the God of peace himself sanctify you completely, and may your whole spirit and soul and body be kept blameless at the coming of our Lord Jesus Christ" (1 Thess. 5:23–24). Like our glorification, this is a divine work: "He who calls you is faithful; he will surely do it" (v. 24).

A Matter of Faith, Not Sight

As we have seen, we are being glorified by degrees in this life. This reality is not an obvious one. It is matter of faith, not sight. What Alister McGrath says about Martin Luther's theology of the cross is relevant to our topic. McGrath points out that for Luther, God was at work in the cross to save, but his presence and work were not obvious. They were hidden but real.[25] Likewise, God's work of glorifying us is not obvious but hidden. We walk by faith, not by sight.[26] This is why Paul could write about our being transformed from one degree of glory to another (2 Cor. 3:18). Yet he could also write in the same letter that while our outer nature is wasting away, our inner nature is being renewed every day (2 Cor. 4:16–18).

Conclusion

Our glorification is a Trinitarian work. It has two phases. The first phase begins in the here and now. It is a process. The second phase is an event: final transformation into a glorious being like Christ. However, soberingly, Christ suffered

25. Alister McGrath, *A Cloud of Witnesses: Ten Great Christian Thinkers* (Leicester: Inter-Varsity Press, 1990), 62–65.

26. The great contrast in Scripture is between faith and sight, not faith and reason (2 Cor. 5:7). In fact, God invites his people to reason with him: "Come now, let us reason together, says the Lord" (Isa. 1:18). And Jesus used common forms of logical argument. For examples, we find both *a fortiori* (Matt. 7:11) and *reductio ad absurdum* in the Gospels (e.g., Mark 3:23–27).

before entering his glory. For many Christians today, suffering is very much their experience. In some parts of the world, to be Christian is to invite persecution and even death. I recall a table conversation between a Nigerian theological student and a Pakistani one. I listened in (I was one of their professors). They would soon be graduating and were talking about their prospects. The Nigerian student expected physical beatings from Muslims, and the Pakistani one spoke of being killed for his faith in Christ.

Excursus: The Lord Is the Spirit

Paul's assertion "This comes from the Lord who is the Spirit" in 2 Corinthians 3:18 raises some deep theological questions. Is Paul collapsing the second and third persons of the triune Godhead into one person? Some argue so. For example, theologian Hendrikus Berkhof argues from verse 18 that the risen Christ becomes the Spirit: "The work of the Spirit is also frequently presented as the work of the exalted Christ himself. . . . In the resurrection he becomes 'a life-giving Spirit' and therefore does not leave us as orphans but comes again to us."[27] The theological cost of this move is extremely high. The doctrine of the essential Trinity is lost, and a form of modalism takes its place. (Modalism argues that God is only an apparent Trinity, and in reality, Father, Son, and Spirit are the one and the same God in different, successive modes of historical activity.) Is this a defensible position? Hardly, given how 2 Corinthians ends.

We read in 2 Corinthians 13:14, "The grace of the Lord Jesus Christ and the love of God and the fellowship of the Holy Spirit be with you all." Paul clearly distinguishes the persons

27. Hendrikus Berkhof, *Christian Faith: An Introduction to the Study of the Faith* (Grand Rapids, MI: Eerdmans, 1979), 325.

of the Godhead and does not collapse them into one.[28] This verse also rules out any binitarian interpretation of 2 Corinthians 3:18 (or a modalist one, for that matter). Paul Barnett captures that binitarian reading in these terms: "Does he [Paul] mean that the Lord Jesus and the Spirit are one and the same person? Is he implying that there are two (Father and Lord = Spirit), not three, persons in the Godhead?" Barnett rightly answers, "The famous tripartite 'Grace' with which the letter concludes conclusively supports a trinitarian rather than a binitarian doctrine."[29]

28. Berkhof's argument would also make nonsense of great Trinitarian texts such as Matt. 28:18–20 and the Upper Room Discourse of Jesus, with its teaching about the Paraclete (John 14–16).

29. Barnett, *Message of 2 Corinthians*, 73.

4

Glorification, the Prospect

Some years ago, I attended an autopsy—a sobering experience. The man on the table was about my age at the time, around twenty-five. He was a strong police officer. An experience like that makes you think. Did this man have any kind of hope for life after death? Or did he think that physical death was the final curtain, the end of the show?

Scripture leaves us in no doubt. As Paul wrote to the Corinthians: "In fact Christ has been raised from the dead, the firstfruits of those who have fallen asleep" (1 Cor. 15:20). Hope is vital for the Christian life. Our eschatological horizon is so very different from that of the secularist. Anthony Thiselton rightly argues: "Our hope and confidence cannot be based on the capacities of human beings to survive death and become immortal. Such confidence depends entirely on *God's promise* of resurrection and new creation. Everything depends here on *trust in God*, not self-reliance."[1] The prospect is of nothing less than new heavens and a new earth, for which the groaning

1. Anthony C. Thiselton, *Life after Death: A New Approach to the Last Things* (Grand Rapids, MI: Eerdmans, 2012), xiii, original emphasis.

creation is longing, and with it the revealing of the glorious liberty of the children of God (Rom. 8:18–25). The sphere of glory to come requires the transformation of our bodies (1 Cor. 15:35–58) to become like that of Christ's own glorified body (Phil. 3:20–21).

This chapter will explore the notion of a glorified body, as well as the question as to when that body is received. Is it upon death or at the end of history? With glorification our progressive sanctification is complete (1 Thess. 5:23). We have, therefore, the hope of glory (Col. 1:27). This hope is for nothing less than "an eternal weight of glory" (2 Cor. 4:16–18). In an earlier chapter we considered Christ's glory, but in this one we turn our attention to his glorification and our own.

The Christological Paradigm

As intimated above, Christ's own experience of resurrection and glorification is intimately connected with the prospect of ours. He is the firstfruits. That is to say, he begins the harvest. His resurrection guarantees our own. So the question arises What does Scripture say about Christ's glorification?[2] In brief, the biblical testimony reveals three phases.

Phase 1: The Cross

Crucifixion was an unspeakably awful way to die. So horrid, in fact, that Roman citizens were exempt from it.[3] Yet Jesus experienced it for our sakes. It is striking, then, that Jesus saw the cross as the occasion of his glorification. He turned up-

2. It is worth noting that in the idiom of John's Gospel, Jesus was glorified paradoxically on the cross (13:31); and so Bernard Ramm correctly writes, "The glorification of the cross is followed by the glorification of the resurrection." *Them He Glorified: A Systematic Study of the Doctrine of Glorification* (Grand Rapids, MI: Eerdmans, 1963), 45.

3. On crucifixion and how it was understood at the time of Jesus, see Fleming Rutledge, *The Crucifixion: Understanding the Death of Jesus Christ* (Grand Rapids, MI: Eerdmans, 2015).

side down the conventional understanding of crucifixion entertained in that day.

John's Gospel, in particular, provides us with insights into this first phase of Christ's glorification. John 1:14 speaks of Christ's glory seen by his disciples, but in John 7:39 we learn that Jesus had not yet been glorified. Regarding the former, Jesus's miraculous signs revealed his glory, as John 2:11 states concerning his turning water into wine at Cana. However, regarding future glorification, John tells us that the Spirit had not yet been given because the giving of the Spirit was contingent upon Jesus's glorification. Pentecost was years away. Moreover, John connects Jesus's glorification with a particular timed event, which Jesus termed "my hour." At the wedding feast at Cana, he said that this hour was to come (John 2:4). The note of the coming hour would be struck twice more. Later, during the Feast of Booths, while Jesus was teaching in the temple, officers were sent to arrest him, but his hour had not yet come (John 7:30). John again assures us that no arrest took place at that time because his hour had not come (John 8:20).

Later again, at Passover time, Jesus explicitly connected his hour, his death, and his glorification: "And Jesus answered them, 'The hour has come for the Son of Man to be glorified. Truly, truly, I say to you, unless a grain of wheat falls into the earth and dies, it remains alone; but if it dies, it bears much fruit'" (John 12:23–24). Subsequently, as the foot-washing scene unfolds in the upper room, John informs the reader yet again that Jesus indeed knew that his hour had come (John 13:1). Jesus's words are cryptic, but it is clear that he had his betrayal and cross in mind (John 13:11). Richard Bauckham observes that in John's Gospel, "the narrative moves relentlessly toward Jesus's 'hour.'"[4] Bauckham

---

4. Richard Bauckham, *Gospel of Glory: Major Themes in Johannine Theology* (Grand Rapids, MI: Baker Academic, 2015), 63.

also helps us understand how an event as heinous as crucifixion can be described in glory terms. He argues that in John's theology, glory is "the visible revelation of God's character."[5] From that perspective, the cross is the exhibition of the loving character of the God who so loved the world that he gave his only Son (John 3:16). Bauckham writes, "The cross as the supreme enactment of God's love is also the supreme revelation of his glory—of who he is."[6]

The cross is the occasion of Christ's own glorification and also his glorification of his heavenly Father: "When [Judas, the betrayer] had gone out, Jesus said, 'Now is the Son of Man glorified, and God is glorified in him'" (John 13:31). In fact, it was while praying to his Father that Jesus connected his glorifying the Father and the Father's glorifying him in terms of his hour having come: "When Jesus had spoken these words, he lifted up his eyes to heaven, and said, 'Father, the hour has come; glorify your Son that the Son may glorify you'" (John 17:1). Bernard Ramm comments, "The New Testament represents the cross as the event in which the Father glorifies the Son, and in which the Son glorifies the Father by always obeying the will of the Father, so fulfilling the work of the Father."[7]

Phase 2: The Resurrection

After his resurrection, Jesus appeared more than once to his disciples. His glory was not yet obvious. For example, Mary did not recognize him in the garden. She thought that she was talking to the gardener (John 20:15). Jesus made it clear that he was in transition: "Jesus said to her, 'Do not cling to me, for I have not yet ascended to the Father; but go to my brothers and

---

5. Bauckham, *Gospel of Glory*, 72.
6. Bauckham, *Gospel of Glory*, 73–74.
7. Ramm, *Them He Glorified*, 44.

say to them, "I am ascending to my Father and your Father, to my God and your God""" (John 20:17).

On the road to Emmaus, the two disciples did not recognize the one who joined them on the road: "While they were talking and discussing together, Jesus himself drew near and went with them. But their eyes were kept from recognizing him" until he broke bread with them (Luke 24:15–16, 30–31). There was something in the way he broke bread that alerted them to his identity.

His resurrection body was different. He could pass through walls, as he did in the room where the disciples were in hiding (John 20:19). However, there was continuity between his resurrection body and his pre-resurrection body because he bore the scars of crucifixion, as Thomas learned in dramatic fashion (John 20:24–27). Other disciples had to learn the same lesson. Luke relates the story of startled disciples thinking the risen Christ was a spirit. Jesus pointed to his scarred body to convince them otherwise (Luke 24:36–37). A spirit, he argued, does not have flesh and bones (Luke 24:39). He even had a meal with them (Luke 24:41–42; Acts 10:40–41).[8] The scars of crucifixion represent no defect in Christ's resurrection body. As Thomas Aquinas argued, "The scars that remained in Christ's body belong neither to corruption nor defect, but to the greater increase of glory, inasmuch as they are the trophies of His power; and a special comeliness will appear in the places scarred by the wounds."[9]

---

8. That Jesus ate and drank with his disciples is intriguing, given the eschatological prospect of the marriage feast of the Lamb (cf. Mark 14:25 and Rev. 19:9). Was his eating and drinking with his disciples, after the resurrection but before the ascension, anticipating the feast to come? Donald G. Bloesch makes the interesting point, regarding the world to come, "We should note that the purpose of food and drink is not merely for sustenance but for fellowship as well." *Essentials of Evangelical Theology*, vol. 2, *Life, Ministry, and Hope* (New York: Harper & Row, 1979), 229. Regarding Mark 14:25, how much is word picture and how much is literal is a fascinating question, but beyond the scope of this work.

9. Thomas Aquinas, *Summa theologiae*, III, Q. 54, Art. 4, New Advent (website), http://www.newadvent.org/, accessed November 11, 2019. In the same place, Aquinas

Phase 3: The Ascension

Jesus is now at the right hand of the Father. He is a glorious figure. In John's vison on Patmos, the heavenly Christ is so glorious that language is stretched to the breaking point as John tries to capture Christ's majestic person: "The hairs of his head were white, like white wool, like snow. His eyes were like a flame of fire, his feet were like burnished bronze, refined in a furnace, and his voice was like the roar of many waters" (Rev. 1:14–15). Little wonder, then, that John was overwhelmed by the sight: "When I saw him, I fell at his feet as though dead" (Rev. 1:17).

Paul instructed the Philippians that our bodies will be transformed to be like Christ's glorious body (Phil. 3:21). This should not surprise us if we are indeed members of his body, animated by the same Holy Spirit who animated and presumably still animates his humanity. For according to Paul, that humanity has not been left behind. Paul preached to the Athenians that God has appointed a man by whom he will judge the world (Acts 17:30–31). The ascended Christ not only is truly God but also remains truly human.

Our Ontological Prospect

Ontology has to do with being. Our ontological prospect has to do with our future being. The apostle Paul had to consider the ontological prospect in dealing with strange notions about the resurrection affecting the church at Corinth. Some at Corinth were denying that Christ had risen (1 Cor. 15:12), and some were even being baptized on behalf of the dead (1 Cor. 15:29). Paul anticipated a possible question then answered it. In so doing he provided the most thorough biblical delineation of the ontological prospect awaiting believers (1 Cor. 15:35–49).

---

also speculated, as did Augustine, whom he quoted, that the martyrs will also still carry their scars as trophies in the kingdom to come.

First, the question: "But someone will ask, 'How are the dead raised? With what kind of body do they come?'" (v. 35). Paul's initial response is strong, "You foolish person!" (v. 36). But he does not leave it there. He turns to the observable world and launches into argument: "What you sow does not come to life unless it dies. And what you sow is not the body that is to be, but a bare kernel, perhaps of wheat or of some other grain" (vv. 36–37). The apostle doesn't stop with the vegetable kingdom. He develops the argument: "But God gives it a body as he has chosen, and to each kind of seed its own body. For not all flesh is the same, but there is one kind for humans, another for animals, another for birds, and another for fish" (vv. 38–39).

Next, he extends the canvas and introduces the note of glory: "There are heavenly bodies and earthly bodies, but the glory of the heavenly is of one kind, and the glory of the earthly is of another. There is one glory of the sun, and another glory of the moon, and another glory of the stars; for star differs from star in glory" (vv. 40–41).

At this point, the Corinthians may have been wondering where Paul was heading. The point soon comes:

> So is it with the resurrection of the dead. What is sown is perishable; what is raised is imperishable. It is sown in dishonor; it is raised in glory. It is sown in weakness; it is raised in power. It is sown a natural body; it is raised a spiritual body. If there is a natural body, there is also a spiritual body. (vv. 42–44)[10]

Paul develops his argument for the resurrection in terms of Scripture, Christology, and anthropology (vv. 45–49). He appeals to the Genesis narrative: "Thus it is written, 'The first

---

10. In Matt. 22:30, while debating with the Sadducees, who denied the resurrection, Jesus argued that with our resurrection we will be like the angels in heaven. In context, he was talking about marriage and being given in marriage. He was not talking about our ontology. We will not become spirits like the angels (Heb. 1:14).

man Adam became a living being'; the last Adam became a life-giving spirit" (1 Cor. 15:45; cf. Gen. 2:7). Paul follows the narrative flow of redemptive history: "But it is not the spiritual that is first but the natural, and then the spiritual. The first man was from the earth, a man of dust; the second man is from heaven" (1 Cor. 15:46–47). Next, he brings us into the picture: "As was the man of dust, so also are those who are of the dust, and as is the man of heaven, so also are those who are of heaven. Just as we have borne the image of the man of dust, we shall also bear the image of the man of heaven" (vv. 48–49). The apostle is a synthetic thinker. He knows how to draw things together, and in so doing he makes it clear that our destiny is tied to Christ's own.

Just when will this all take place? This must have been on the minds of the Corinthians, since some of them had already died because of their abuse of the Lord's Supper (1 Cor. 11:30: "some have died"). Moreover, the practice of some at Corinth in being baptized for the dead may have also raised the question (1 Cor. 15:29). Paul lays down a principle: "I tell you this, brothers: flesh and blood cannot inherit the kingdom of God, nor does the perishable inherit the imperishable" (1 Cor. 15:50). He then makes an appeal to mystery. Mystery for Paul is not something spooky but some element in the plan of God once hidden and now revealed: "Behold! I tell you a mystery. We shall not all sleep, but we shall all be changed, in a moment, in the twinkling of an eye, at the last trumpet. For the trumpet will sound, and the dead will be raised imperishable, and we shall be changed" (1 Cor. 15:51–52). What kind of change? Paul writes:

> For this perishable body must put on the imperishable, and this mortal body must put on immortality. When the perishable puts on the imperishable, and the mortal

puts on immortality, then shall come to pass the saying that is written:

> "Death is swallowed up in victory."
>> "O death, where is your victory?
>> O death, where is your sting?"

The sting of death is sin, and the power of sin is the law. But thanks be to God, who gives us the victory through our Lord Jesus Christ. (1 Cor. 15:53–57)

So What?

Paul was a pastor. He could not leave great truths unapplied. The end of chapter 15 draws out the logical implications of his argument: "Therefore, my beloved brothers, be steadfast, immovable, always abounding in the work of the Lord, knowing that in the Lord your labor is not in vain" (v. 58). The apostle models what responsible application looks like in a particular pastoral context. No resurrection, no hope. He has already made the point in verse 32 by quoting from Isaiah 22:13: "What do I gain if, humanly speaking, I fought with beasts at Ephesus? If the dead are not raised, 'Let us eat and drink, for tomorrow we die.'" This pessimism coincided with the Epicurean philosophy prevalent at the time Paul wrote.[11] But with Christ's own resurrection comes hope for our own transformation.

When?

The traditional theological view is that upon death the believer enters an intermediate state as a disembodied spirit awaiting the

---

11. See the discussion in Anthony C. Thiselton, *The First Epistle to the Corinthians: A Commentary on the Greek Text*, The New International Greek Testament Commentary (Grand Rapids, MI: Eerdmans, 2000), 1252–53.

general resurrection of the body.[12] Murray J. Harris states the traditional view accurately:

> The expression "the intermediate state" is not found in Scripture, but in Christian theology it traditionally refers to the condition of all mankind between death and resurrection or to the period that elapses (from an early viewpoint) between the death of the individual and the consummation of history. This condition is called "intermediate" because it lies between two fixed points, death and resurrection, and because it is temporary, ultimately eclipsed by the "final state" of humankind.[13]

This is the paradise that Jesus promised the penitent thief on the cross: "And he said, 'Jesus, remember me when you come into your kingdom.' And he said to him, 'Truly, I say to you, today you will be with me in paradise'" (Luke 23:42–43).

What makes even a disembodied state a paradise is that the believer is with his or her Lord. Paul strikes this note with the Philippians: "If I am to live in the flesh, that means fruitful labor for me. Yet which I shall choose I cannot tell. I am hard pressed between the two. My desire is to depart and be with Christ, for that is far better" (Phil. 1:22–23). Michael Horton states this view well:

> The body apart from the soul is dead (Jas 2:26), yet for believers, to be absent from the body is to be present with

12. Some scholars argue that a disembodied existence was an impossible thought for first-century Jews. However, 2 Cor. 12:2–3 reveals that Paul was a first-century Jew who could contemplate a conscious existence without his body: "whether in the body or out of the body I do not know."

13. Murray J. Harris, *From Grave to Glory: Resurrection in the New Testament; Including a Response to Norman L. Geisler* (Grand Rapids, MI: 1990), 206. In the 1980s, there was much controversy over Harris's view of the resurrection. Geisler took issue with it, accusing Harris of heresy. In the end, Harris prevailed and was judged by the relevant denomination (Evangelical Free Church of America) and its school (Trinity Evangelical Divinity School) as not heretical but having a view that fell within the bounds of orthodoxy. The issue was not on the resurrection per se; both Harris and Geisler affirmed that unequivocally. The issue was the nature of the resurrection body. See the article by Scot McKnight, "The Nature of Bodily Resurrection: A Debatable Issue," *Journal of the Evangelical Theological Society* 33, no. 3 (1990): 379–82.

the Lord (2 Cor 5:8). Neither the everlasting consummation nor unconsciousness, this intermediate state is God's
preservation of the personal consciousness of believers in
his presence awaiting the resurrection of the dead.[14]

Death separates. At the resurrection of the dead, a great reunion
will take place between soul and body. This is a far cry from the
ancient pagan view of the body as a prison for the soul from
which it needs to escape (e.g., Platonism). As both the Bible and
the great creeds (Apostles' and Nicene) teach, we believe in the
resurrection of the body.

One variant of this traditional view comes with a premillen-
nial eschatology. On this view, the disembodied saints receive
embodiment for the millennium in order to rule with Christ.
This is a period in which the martyrs in particular are singled
out by God for vindication. Revelation 20:1–6 speaks of a thou-
sand-year reign of Christ on the earth. Premillennialists believe
that this is to be taken either as a literal thousand years or as a
period of time symbolized as a thousand years. On both views,
the earth is the setting, and the general resurrection and last
judgment are still to come beyond it. Russell Moore articulates
this view well in its historic premillennialist form:

> Historic premillennialism fits best with a natural exegesis of
> Revelation 20; the first and second resurrections are both
> bodily—one of the righteous at the beginning of the millen-
> nium and one of the unrighteous at the end, a resurrection
> identified with the second death. It fits the flow of Revela-
> tion, coming after the climax of the book with the coming
> of Christ and before the eternal state.[15]

---

14. Michael Horton, *The Christian Faith: A Systematic Theology for Pilgrims on the
Way* (Grand Rapids, MI: Zondervan, 2011), 912–13.

15. Russell D. Moore, "Personal and Cosmic Eschatology," in *A Theology for the
Church*, ed. Daniel L. Akin, rev. ed. (Nashville: B&H, 2014), 710. Strictly speaking,
Moore posits two resurrections, when in actual fact Revelation speaks of one resurrection

Still another variant is that upon death, the believer receives the resurrection body, and thus there is no disembodied intermediate state. This view depends upon the idea that Paul's eschatology underwent development from 1 Corinthians 15 to 2 Corinthians 5. David E. Garland appears to hold this view, but with some tentativeness, when he writes:

> Nakedness, some incorporeal existence, is an absurd idea to him because of the resurrection of Christ; and his assertion that we will not be found naked links with his earlier insistence in 1 Cor 15:35–44 that "the future life is a bodily one." If we prune away the metaphorical language in this verse, Paul simply says that the dead rise with a body. If this is correct, we should not read into his imagery an interim period or an interim state. Nor should we read into this verse any dread of some naked state. Instead, this assertion should be understood as expressing the solace that Paul's resurrection hope gives him: "we shall not be found naked."[16]

However, apart from the difficulty of Paul abandoning an earlier view of his and what that would mean for biblical authority, there are a number of reasons for holding to the traditional view of an intermediate state. Murray Harris argues cogently that this nontraditional view undermines the tension that pervades the Epistles between the already (our present existence) and the not yet (the parousia). This tension is explicit in 1 Corinthians 15. Harris writes:

---

at the end of the millennium, which is described as the first (Rev. 20:5–6). He assumes that the souls who come to life are embodied (Rev. 20:4). An amillennialist would dissent and read Rev. 20 with the reign of Christ as a spiritual reality through the church and the first resurrection as the regeneration of the believer. On either view, the resurrection of the body is affirmed. This is also the case with other eschatological positions: classic dispensationalism, progressive dispensationalism, and postmillennialism.

16. David E. Garland, *2 Corinthians*, The New American Commentary (Nashville: Broadman & Holman, 1999), 260.

To place the resurrection of the body at death is to rob the parousia of its temporal significance, do less than justice to the corporate emphases of Pauline eschatology, and remove the tension between the "already" and the "not yet" that characterizes the entire period between the two advents of Christ.[17]

Our Vocational Prospect

It is striking to observe the symmetry between protology and eschatology with regard to human vocation before God. Protology, which deals with the first things, reveals that the vocation of Adam and Eve was to be king/queen and priests.[18] They were to exercise dominion and subdue the earth like a king and queen, and in so doing they would image the ultimate Ruler of all things, God.

> So God created man in his own image,
> in the image of God he created him;
> male and female he created them.

> And God blessed them. And God said to them, "Be fruitful and multiply and fill the earth and subdue it, and have dominion over the fish of the sea and over the birds of the heavens and over every living thing that moves on the earth." (Gen. 1:27–28)

Our first parents were also to care for the garden, which was a sacred space, like priests. In the first instance the role

17. Murray J. Harris, *The Second Epistle to the Corinthians: A Commentary on the Greek Text*, The New International Greek Testament Commentary (Grand Rapids, MI: Eerdmans; Milton Keynes, UK: Paternoster, 2005), 378. Harris gives four other rebuttals of this revisionist view of when we receive the resurrection body. I commend his fuller argument to the reader.

18. The phrase "king/queen" is a tad awkward, but it is my attempt to capture the thrust of the biblical text (Gen. 1:26–28) where the mandate to rule is addressed to both male and female.

was given to Adam: "The LORD God took the man and put him in the garden of Eden to work it and keep it" (Gen. 2:15).[19] Both these roles reappear at the very end of the biblical canon. On the new earth, God's people are to serve him as priests and to rule as kings and queens.

> No longer will there be anything accursed, but the throne of God and of the Lamb will be in it, and his servants will worship him [as priests do]. They will see his face, and his name will be on their foreheads. And night will be no more. They will need no light of lamp or sun, for the Lord God will be their light, and they will reign [as rulers do] forever and ever.[20] (Rev. 22:3–5)

The cultural mandate as found in Genesis 1:27–28 and subsequently disrupted by sin (Gen. 3), and then recovered in and through Christ for us (Heb. 2:5–9), has its quintessential expression in the realm of the new earth (Rev. 22:3–5).

The testimony of protology and eschatology fits well with Haley Goranson Jacob's thesis that glorification in Romans 8 is to be understood in vocational terms. She writes:

> Being united with Christ, believers thus participate in the resurrection life of Christ; they actively share with Christ in his messianic and new Adamic reign. This motif of vocational participation in Jesus' reign arises again in Romans 8:17, where Paul describes it in terms of being co-inheritors and coglorified with the Son. On the basis of believers' adoption to sonship (Rom 8:14–16) and thus their change in identity, as children of God believers participate with the Son of God in his inheritance and

---

19. This language ("work" and "keep") is later in the Pentateuch predicated of the Levitical priests.

20. Rev. 22:3–5 is clearly not restricted to males.

glory—his vocational rule over the world as the Firstborn Son of God.[21]

Her summation is this: "Believers' final glorification in Romans is their reinstatement to Adamic rule over creation through union with the Firstborn Son of God, who already reigns over creation as the Messiah and the new Adam."[22] The note of sharing in Christ's rule both in the present and in the future consummation is very evident in Romans, as Jacob correctly argues. John has the same accent in Revelation 22, but adds the priestly one.

The Honor Prospect

To glorify another person is to honor that person. This can be done by word (e.g., praise) and by deed (e.g., bestowing a crown). In the famous Sermon on the Mount, Jesus teaches that his followers can expect rewards for faithfulness in heaven: "Blessed are you when others revile you and persecute you and utter all kinds of evil against you falsely on my account. Rejoice and be glad, for your reward is great in heaven, for so they persecuted the prophets who were before you" (Matt. 5:11–12). Treasures can be laid up in heaven, according to Jesus (Matt. 6:19–20). In the Parable of the Talents, Jesus speaks of faithful servants who do as the master has instructed and in so doing reap his praise: "His master said to him, 'Well done, good and faithful servant. You have been faithful over a little; I will set you over much. Enter into the joy of your master'" (Matt. 25:21). The apostle Paul wrote to the Colossians of an inheritance as their reward: "Whatever you do, work heartily, as for the Lord and not for men, knowing that from the Lord

---

21. Haley Goranson Jacob, *Conformed to the Image of His Son: Reconsidering Paul's Theology of Glory in Romans* (Downers Grove, IL: IVP Academic, 2018), 259.
22. Jacob, *Conformed to the Image*, 264.

you will receive the inheritance as your reward. You are serv-
ing the Lord Christ" (Col. 3:23–24). Paul himself expected a
"crown of righteousness" to be bestowed on him (2 Tim. 4:8).
Paul also taught that there will be a judgment of believers at the
judgment seat of Christ: "So whether we are at home or away,
we make it our aim to please him. For we must all appear before
the judgment seat of Christ, so that each one may receive what
is due for what he has done in the body, whether good or evil"
(2 Cor. 5:9–10). At issue is not salvation, but service.

Herman Bavinck provides an excellent summary of the biblical evidence concerning degrees of glory in the world to come. He
maintains: "Such degrees of distinction in glory are taught much
more clearly in other passages in Scripture [he has been discussing Matt. 20:1–16], especially those stating that all [he is speaking of believers] will receive a reward commensurate with their
works."[23] He gives extensive biblical support for the following
claims: "That reward is now kept in heaven (Matt. 5:12; 6:1ff.;
Luke 6:23; 1 Tim. 6:19; Heb. 10:34–37) and will be publicly
distributed only at the parousia (Matt. 6:4, 6, 18; 24:47; 2 Thess.
1:7; 1 Pet. 4:13)."[24] He cites a variety of scriptures to establish
that rewards will be commensurate with works: "That reward
will be linked with and proportionate to the works performed
(Matt. 16:27; 19:29; 25:21, 23; Luke 6:38; 19:17, 19; Rom. 2:6;
1 Cor. 3:8; 2 Cor. 4:17; 5:10; 9:6; Gal. 6:8–9; Heb. 11:26; Rev.
2:23; 11:18; 20:12; 22:12)."[25] The question arises as to how the
degrees of glory will manifest themselves. Bavinck supplies an
answer: "Blessedness is indeed the same for all, but there are distinctions in 'brightness' and glory (Dan. 12:3; 1 Cor. 15:41)."[26]

23. Herman Bavinck, *Reformed Dogmatics: Abridged into One Volume*, ed. John
Bolt (Grand Rapids, MI: Baker Academic, 2011), 776. No translator is indicated.
    24. Bavinck, *Reformed Dogmatics: Abridged*, 776.
    25. Bavinck, *Reformed Dogmatics: Abridged*, 776.
    26. Bavinck, *Reformed Dogmatics: Abridged*, 776.

The Home for the Glorified

A common way to sum up the flow of the biblical story is in terms of four categories: creation, fall, redemption, and consummation.[27] In other words, Scripture has a plot, and as Aristotle said, a plot has "a beginning, middle and end."[28] A plot takes you on a journey, as does Scripture. Regarding the consummation, or the end, a more granular question to ask is What does the home of the glorified look like? I imagine that if churchgoers were asked what is the final home for God's people, most would answer, "heaven." The French Protestant Simon Goulart (1543–1628) was effusive in describing this prospect at the conclusion of his *Christian Discourses*, volume 1. The descriptors are so magnificent that extensive quotation is in order:

> The eternal and blessed life with God in heaven, accompanied by rest and unspeakable glory, is the goal of the faith of Christians. This is the harbor of their hope, the refuge of all their desires, the crown of their consolation that they will certainly enjoy, having escaped from the travails of this miserable and fleeting earthly life, indeed, from death itself.[29]

Goulart elaborates:

> They will receive in heaven . . . glorified bodies, healed of all evils, no longer afflicted by sin, ignorance, errors, illness, sadness, worry, fear, anguish, or enemies. They will be delivered from all pain and suffering. They will enjoy fully and completely the Lord their God, the fountain and

---

27. E.g., John Stott, *Issues Facing Christians Today*, 4th ed. (Grand Rapids, MI: Zondervan, 2006), 82.

28. Aristotle, *Poetics*, trans. S. H. Butcher (Mineola, NY: Dover, 1997), 14.

29. In Scott M. Manetsch, *Calvin's Company of Pastors: Pastoral Care and the Emerging Reformed Church, 1536–1609* (Oxford, UK: Oxford University Press, 2012), 297. I am so grateful for Dr. Manetsch's drawing my attention to this material.

inexhaustible treasure of all good things, who will pour out on them all his goodness, his infinite joy, with which he will satisfy all their thoughts and desires. They will see him and contemplate him face to face, without any clouds to obscure him. They will learn of God's wisdom with regard to the creation and redemption of his elect by means of Jesus Christ, and the reasons for his all-powerful and wondrous works. The eternal Father will disclose his burning and unspeakable love for them, which he demonstrated by sending his Son into the world to draw them from death into eternal life. His children will be moved by his gracious work, filled with wonder, contentment, and ineffable delight, and will love their heavenly Father with a burning love, submitting themselves fully to his wisdom with eager joy. And they will submit to him as their only sovereign and greatest good. And they will rejoice with continuous joy in his presence, magnifying his glory, singing of his goodness along with the holy Angels and the entire Church triumphant. There they will see Jesus Christ, the blessed virgin Mother, the Patriarchs, the Prophets, the Apostles, and all the faithful who have preceded them, including their family members and friends who died in repentance and faith. This entire company together, with one heart and voice, will recall the goodness and infinite blessings God has shown them, celebrating with songs of thanksgiving the praises of the Father, the Son, and the Holy Spirit. . . .

Thus, eternal life is the end and fulfillment of all good things, for which God has purchased us through his Son. This is the goal on which our gaze should be fixed throughout our earthly pilgrimage. This is the treasure that we should unceasingly desire. This is the hour and the blessing to which all the plans and efforts of our lives should be inclined. . . . This is our true country, our permanent city, in which our citizenship has been acquired by the merit of the death of Jesus Christ. This is the home that we long for, amidst the banishments, the weariness, the dangerous fears of this valley of misery and the shadow of death. This is the safe refuge and the beautiful harbor toward which we sail amidst so many waves and storms that constantly trouble the world. This is the blessed land where we will dwell by means of death.[30]

Goulart's description of the life to come is so right, except for where he has located it. Heaven is penultimate, not ultimate. Indeed, preoccupation with heaven can be a sign of arrested eschatological development. The final home for God's people is the new earth and the Jerusalem that has come down out of heaven to the renewed earth (Rev. 21:1–2). Russell Moore again puts it well: "The point of the gospel is not that we go to heaven when we die. Instead, it is that heaven will come down, transforming and renewing the earth and the entire universe."[31] Happily, a number of its features are revealed in the biblical text.[32]

Its Description

The world to come is described in various ways. Paul refers to our inheritance in more than one place in Ephesians (1:11, 18; 5:5). He also refers to the future world as "a kingdom to be inherited" (1 Cor. 6:9–10). Peter likewise speaks of an inheritance yet future (1 Pet. 1:3–5). He also describes it as the new heavens and the new earth in which righteousness is at home (2 Pet. 3:13). Hebrews uses a variety of images to refer to this

---

30. In Manetsch, *Calvin's Company of Pastors*, 297–98.
31. Moore, "Personal and Cosmic Eschatology," 711.
32. See Oren R. Martin, *Bound for the Promised Land: The Land of Promise in God's Redemptive Plan*, New Studies in Biblical Theology (Nottingham, UK: Apollos; Downers Grove, IL: IVP Academic, 2015), 56–58; 153–57.

glorious future for God's people. It is "a homeland" (11:14), "a better country" (11:16), "a heavenly one" (11:16), and "a city" (11:16). Bernard Ramm rightly contends that "the process of glorification is not complete until the believer enters into a state of glorious existence within the New Jerusalem."[33]

Its Purpose

Home is where our richest relationships are to be found. Scripture reveals that the divine intention has always been relationship, communion, fellowship. In the garden, God walked with his image bearers (Gen. 3:8). His glorious presence dwelt first in the tabernacle (Ex. 40:34) and then in the temple (1 Kings 8:10–11). That is to say, God dwelt in the midst of his people. Supremely, he pitched his tent among us as the incarnate one (John 1:14). And the promise of his presence is reaffirmed right at the very end of the canon as the centerpiece of the world to come: "the throne of God and the Lamb" (Rev. 22:1). We see in Revelation 21:1–3 nothing less than the realization of the covenant refrain that first appears in Exodus 6:7: "I will take you to be my people, and I will be your God, and you shall know that I am the LORD your God, who has brought you out from under the burdens of the Egyptians." The promise is reaffirmed in the prophets: "For this is the covenant that I will make with the house of Israel after those days, declares the LORD: I will put my law within them, and I will write it on their hearts. And I will be their God, and they shall be my people" (Jer. 31:33). That same promise is reasserted as Paul quotes Jeremiah (2 Cor. 6:16). Hebrews does likewise in Hebrews 8:10. How extraordinary it is that the Creator of all things desires fellowship with such creatures as us. Furthermore, God does so not as to mere servants but as to his children (1 John 3:1–2).

---

33. Ramm, *Them He Glorified*, 116.

Its Activity: Priestly and Royal

The early chapters of Genesis, the first book in the canon, are clear as to the task of God's image bearers. Humankind is to image God by exercising dominion as rulers do and serve their Creator as priests do. The last book in the canon of Scripture shows the recovery of both tasks. In Revelation 1:5–6 there is a doxological (praise) note: "To him who loves us and has freed us from our sins by his blood and made us a kingdom, priests to his God and Father, to him be glory and dominion forever and ever. Amen." "Kingdom" implies kings. The priestly note is explicit.[34] Next, Revelation 5:10 adds the location of the reign of believers: "And you have made them a kingdom and priests to our God, and they shall reign on the earth." The climax of the royal and priestly accents is found in the very last chapter of the book:

> No longer will there be anything accursed, but the throne of God and of the Lamb will be in it [the city of God], and his servants will worship him [the priestly]. They will see his face, and his name will be on their foreheads. And night will be no more. They will need no light of lamp or sun, for the Lord God will be their light, and they will reign forever and ever [the royal]. (Rev. 22:3–4)

Hope has given way to sight: "They will see his face" (v. 4; cf. 1 John 3:1–3). Citing these three texts from Revelation, Herman Bavinck argues with reference to believers in the world to come: "They are prophets, priests, and kings who reign on earth forever (1:6; 5:10; 22:5)."[35] However, as we have seen, the prophetic task is absent from the very texts he cites. Why is

---

34. For an illuminating treatment of the motifs of ruler and priest in Gen. 1–2 and Rev. 21–22, see William J. Dumbrell, *The End of the Beginning: Revelation 21–22 and the Old Testament* (Eugene, OR: Wipf & Stock, 2001), 175–79.

35. Bavinck, *Reformed Dogmatics: Abridged*, 775.

this so? I suggest it is because the prophetic task is to address fallen humanity with revelation from God, often with judgment in mind. In the world to come, that task is no longer needed.

Clearly the end-time picture does not depict a place of indolence. Moore writes, "Eternity means civilization, architecture, banquet feasting, ruling, work—in short, it is eternal *life.*"[36] The world to come won't be a place of boredom either. In his book *Death and the Afterlife*, Paul Williamson makes this valuable observation regarding Revelation 22:1–5:

> Some readers may be relieved to see no mention of endless singing or perpetual harp playing. The text neglects to say exactly [I would prefer to say "expansively" since we will be kings and priests] how we will occupy ourselves in this new creation, but we can rule out the possibility of boredom in a perfected physical realm filled with all the majesty and splendour of God.[37]

The world to come is where believers will be with Jesus their Lord. That will be boring only if Jesus is, and that is unthinkable.

Its Beauty

In philosophy there are three qualities of being that are referred to as the transcendentals: goodness, truth, and beauty. All three apply to the God of the Bible, as the book of Psalms eloquently shows. The Lord is good (34:8). The Lord delights in truth (51:6). The Lord is beautiful (27:4). Given the beauty of God, it is no surprise that the city of God too is described as beautiful: "And he carried me away in the Spirit to a great, high mountain, and showed me the holy city Jerusalem coming down out of heaven from God,

---

36. Moore, "Personal and Cosmic Eschatology," 711.
37. Paul R. Williamson, *Death and the Afterlife: Biblical Perspectives on Ultimate Questions* (Downers Grove, IL: IVP Academic, 2018), 189.

having the glory of God, its radiance like a most rare jewel, like a jasper, clear as crystal" (Rev. 21:10–11). The seer elaborates:

> The wall was built of jasper, while the city was pure gold, like clear glass. The foundations of the wall of the city were adorned with every kind of jewel. The first was jasper, the second sapphire, the third agate, the fourth emerald, the fifth onyx, the sixth carnelian, the seventh chrysolite, the eighth beryl, the ninth topaz, the tenth chrysoprase, the eleventh jacinth, the twelfth amethyst. And the twelve gates were twelve pearls, each of the gates made of a single pearl, and the street of the city was pure gold, like transparent glass. (Rev. 21:18–21)

Michael Wilcock rightly sees the significance of these descriptors when he comments, "Lastly the beauty of new Jerusalem is portrayed: walls encrusted with precious stones, every gate a single pearl, the buildings and open spaces of the city made of an inconceivable crystal-clear gold. With this glittering splendor God completes his preparation of 'the Bride, the wife of the Lamb.'"[38]

The world to come is anything but dull and drab. How can it be if Jesus is there?

Its Cultural Wealth

The last book of the Bible is full of passages that fascinate. Revelation 21:24–26 is one such passage. The city of God is illuminated by the glory of God, and its lamp is the Lamb of God. Hence, there is no need for sun or moon (Rev. 21:23). Then we read: "By its light will the nations walk, and the kings of the earth will bring their glory into it, and its gates

---

38. Michael Wilcock, *The Message of Revelation: I Saw Heaven Opened*, The Bible Speaks Today (Downers Grove, IL: InterVarsity Press, 1986), 209.

will never be shut by day—and there will be no night there. They will bring into it the glory and the honor of the nations." (vv. 24–26). What can this mean? Craig Bartholomew and Michael Goheen are in doubt as to its meaning but offer this outlook: "The cultural achievements of history will be purified and will reappear on the new earth (Revelation 21:24–26)."[39] Wilcock elaborates, "'The glory and the honor of the nations' contribute to the magnificence of the city; all that is truly good and beautiful in this world will reappear there, purified and enhanced in the perfect setting its Maker intended for it; nothing of real value is lost."[40]

Its Holiness

Paul is adamant that the sinful will not find a place in the kingdom of God. He informs the Corinthians accordingly:

> Or do you not know that the unrighteous will not inherit the kingdom of God? Do not be deceived: neither the sexually immoral, nor idolaters, nor adulterers, nor men who practice homosexuality, nor thieves, nor the greedy, nor drunkards, nor revilers, nor swindlers will inherit the kingdom of God. (1 Cor. 6:9–10)

Revelation makes a similar claim with reference to those who find no place in the coming city of God, the new Jerusalem: "Outside are the dogs and sorcerers and the sexually immoral

39. Craig G. Bartholomew and Michael W. Goheen, *The Drama of Scripture: Finding Our Place in the Biblical Story* (Grand Rapids, MI: Baker Academic, 2004), 213. This was apparently also Abraham Kuyper's view (see Bartholomew and Goheen, *Drama of Scripture*, 232n12).

40. Wilcock, *The Message of Revelation*, 211. For a contra view, see Gregory K. Beale, *The Book of Revelation: A Commentary on the Greek Text*, The New International Greek Testament Commentary (Grand Rapids, MI: Eerdmans; Carlisle, UK: Paternoster, 1999), 1096: "Consequently, 'glory and honor' probably refer not to literal riches but to riches as a picture of the nations' absolute, wholehearted subservience to God." Since so much of Rev. 21 is about the splendor of the city of God, "a bride adorned for her husband" (v. 2), I am more convinced by Bartholomew and Goheen than by Beale.

and murderers and idolaters, and everyone who loves and practices falsehood" (Rev. 22:15).

The Jerusalem come down from heaven is pictured as a cubical space:

> And the one who spoke with me had a measuring rod of gold to measure the city and its gates and walls. The city lies foursquare, its length the same as its width. And he measured the city with his rod, 12,000 stadia [a *stadion* is about 1,380–1,400 miles]. Its length and width and height are equal. (Rev. 21:15–16)

Kendell H. Easley sees the significance of the dimensions:

> The point here is that the New Jerusalem is a perfect cube, which was the exact shape of the inner sanctuary, the Most Holy Place of the Israelite temple (1 Kgs. 6:19). In earthly Jerusalem the glory of God was limited to a single, tiny, cube-shaped room; in New Jerusalem the glory of God fills a vast cube-shaped city.[41]

The cubical nature of the space underlines its holiness.

Conclusion

John Murray is correct when writing of the importance of the biblical teaching on hope: "Life here and now that is not conditioned by faith in Jesus' first coming and oriented to the hope of his second is godless and hopeless."[42] The hope of glory is not for some disembodied ethereal existence. Heaven is penultimate, not ultimate, in the biblical vision of the future. Nothing less than a new heaven and a new earth will do.

41. Kendell H. Easley, *Revelation*, Holman New Testament Commentary (Nashville: Broadman & Holman, 1998), 339.
42. John Murray, "The Advent of Christ," in *The Claims of Truth*, vol. 1 of *Collected Writings of John Murray* (Edinburgh, UK: Banner of Truth, 1976), 94.

The new Jerusalem is terrestrial. As Bernard Ramm writes, "If man's redeemed soul calls for a redeemed body, the redeemed body calls for a redeemed environment."[43] That redeemed environment is the new Jerusalem. It is a glorious city, splendid in beauty. It is a home for which only a glorified people of God would be fit. In the city of God to come, humanity's original calling to rule as kings and queens and serve in worship as priests will find its apogee. In the world to come there will be different degrees of glory for believers in respect to rewards and praise. The degrees of glory are contingent upon faithful service rendered in this life.

Excursus: Like Knows Like

An ancient epistemological principle states that like knows like. E. L. Mascall explains, "Its technical name is 'knowledge by connaturality,' and it is the knowledge which one has by possessing its character oneself."[44] To illustrate this epistemic principle: a person can know another person in a way that my dog cannot know me and I cannot know my dog. We see this principle in Paul's first letter to the Corinthians in the context of an argument about knowing the things of the Spirit. He writes:

> But, as it is written,
>
>> "What no eye has seen, nor ear heard,
>>   nor the heart of man imagined,
>>   what God has prepared for those who love him"—
>
> these things God has revealed to us through the Spirit. For the Spirit searches everything, even the depths of God. For who knows a person's thoughts except the

43. Ramm, *Them He Glorified*, 110.
44. E. L. Mascall, *Grace and Glory* (New York: Morehouse-Barlow, 1961), 43.

spirit of that person, which is in him? So also no one comprehends the thoughts of God except the Spirit of God. (1 Cor. 2:9–11)

Gordon Fee comments: "The basis of the argument will be the Greek philosophical principle of 'like is known only by like,' that is, humans do not on their own possess the quality that would make it possible to know God or God's wisdom. Only 'like is known by like'; only God can know God."[45] Interestingly, in the fourth century there was controversy about the deity of the Holy Spirit. Basil of Caesarea appealed to the connaturality principle to argue that the Holy Spirit is indeed God, citing 1 Corinthians 2:1 as biblical evidence for his claim.[46]

According to Paul, the fullest knowledge of God that we as creatures may acquire lies in the world to come. The apostle Paul wrote to the Corinthians:

For we know in part and we prophesy in part, but when the perfect comes, the partial will pass away. When I was a child, I spoke like a child, I thought like a child, I reasoned like a child. When I became a man, I gave up childish ways. For now we see in a mirror dimly, but then face to face. Now I know in part; then I shall know fully, even as I have been fully known. (1 Cor. 13:9–12)

The "perfect" in this context refers to the world to come.

But how does our glorification fit in here? One ancient philosopher expressed the connaturality principle in this

45. Gordon D. Fee, *God's Empowering Presence: The Holy Spirit in the Letters of Paul* (Peabody, MA: Hendrickson, 2005), 99.
46. Basil the Great, *De Spiritu sancto*, 16:40, New Advent (website), http://www .newadvent.org/, accessed October 29, 2019. Also see the discussion by Michael A. G. Haykin, "Defending the Holy Spirit's Deity: Basil of Caesarea, Gregory of Nyssa, and the Pneumatomachian Controversy of the 4th Century," *Southern Baptist Journal of Theology* 7, no. 3 (2003), https://equip.sbts.edu/, accessed October 30, 2019.

striking way: "To any vision must be brought an eye adapted to what is to be seen, and having some likeness to it. Never did eye see the sun unless it had first become sunlike."[47] I maintain that only as glorified beings can we know as fully as a creature can know the glorious God.

47. Plotinus, *Enneads*, quoted in John E. Lynch, *The Theory of Knowledge of Vital Du Four* (St. Bonaventure, NY: Franciscan Institute, 1972), 151.

Who Will Be Glorified?
Who Will Be Excluded?

Donald Bloesch observes, "While modern thought and theology are ambivalent, if not skeptical, on the question of heaven and hell, the Scriptures are very clear that history will have a twofold outcome."[1] His observation raises the question of who will populate the world to come: Who will constitute the glorified, and who will not? In this chapter, I will discuss both categories and consider an intriguing theory offered by N. T. Wright concerning the fate of those who won't be glorified. But first we turn our attention to the resurrection of the dead, for Scripture is clear that for humankind, whether just or unjust, some kind of embodiment is humankind's destiny. After surveying the beliefs of pagans and Jews in the first-century world, N. T. wright argues forcefully, "Resurrection meant bodies."[2] What we don't find in Scripture is any Platonic notion of fleeing

---

1. Donald G. Bloesch, *Essentials of Evangelical Theology*, vol. 2, *Life, Ministry, and Hope* (New York: Harper & Row, 1979), 211.
2. N. T. Wright, *Surprised by Hope: Rethinking Heaven, the Resurrection, and the Mission of the* Church (New York: Harper-Collins, 2008), 136.

the body to become eternally a bodiless spirit in some kind of afterlife, either for the believer or for the unbeliever.[3]

The Resurrection of the Just and Unjust

The apostle Paul was animated by a great hope. He shared that hope with his captor, Antonius Felix, the Roman governor of Judea:

> But this I confess to you, that according to the Way, which they call a sect, I worship the God of our fathers, believing everything laid down by the Law and written in the Prophets, having a hope in God, which these men themselves accept, that there will be a resurrection of both the just and the unjust. (Acts 24:14–15)

This New Testament belief was so valued by the early church that it found its way into its creeds. For example, the Apostles' Creed climaxes on this eschatological note:

> I believe in . . .
> > the resurrection of the body,
> > and the life everlasting.[4]

Early Christians were prepared to die for this belief. In AD 177, a vicious persecution broke out in Lyons and Vienne in ancient Gaul. Eusebius, the early church historian, preserved a letter from the churches in Gaul that contains this graphic description:

> The bodies, then, of the martyrs, which for six days were displayed and exposed to the elements in every way possible,

---

3. See Christian Irigaray, "Soma Sema: The Body as a Prison for the Soul," Academia, https://www.academia.edu/, accessed December 13, 2019.

4. Question 24 of *To Be a Christian: An Anglican Catechism* (Wheaton, IL: Crossway, 2020), 32.

the lawless men afterwards burnt and reduced to ashes. Then they swept them down to the river Rhone which flows close by, so that not even a trace of them might remain upon the earth. And this they did, thinking that they could conquer God and deprive them of *the regeneration*, "in order," as they themselves said, "that they may not even have hope of a resurrection, in faith of which they introduce into our midst a certain strange and new-fangled cult, and despise dread torments, and are ready to go to their death, and that too with joy. Now let us see if they will rise again, and if their *god can* help them, and *deliver them out of our hands*."[5]

This account shows that the pagans got the message. Christians have a great hope for which they are prepared to suffer torture and die. That hope has to do with the resurrection of the body. J. Stevenson comments, "The belief of the heathen that by destruction of the bodies they could stop resurrection (i.e. of the body) shows the importance of this part of Christian doctrine."[6]

The New Testament affirmation of the resurrection of the just and the unjust shows that the future of humankind is embodiment, whether believers or not.

The Divine Books

The revelation that God keeps a record of names in a book is found in the books of Moses. The golden calf incident at Sinai was an affront to the God who had just rescued his people from Egyptian oppression. Judgment was in order. Moses interceded for the people: "So Moses returned to the Lord and said, 'Alas, this people has sinned a great sin. They have made

---

5. Quoted in J. Stevenson, ed., *A New Eusebius: Documents Illustrative of the History of the Church to A.D. 337* (London: SPCK, 1970), 40, original emphases.
6. Stevenson, *A New Eusebius*, 41n59.

for themselves gods of gold. But now, if you will forgive their sin—but if not, please blot me out of your book that you have written'" (Ex. 32:31–32). God, though, had other plans: "But the LORD said to Moses, 'Whoever has sinned against me, I will blot out of my book'" (Ex. 32:33). Judgment takes the form of a plague (Ex. 32:35).

This is the first mention of a book in the Scriptures. It is a picture that would have been well understood in the ancient Near East, where rulers kept lists in books. Douglas K. Stuart gives illuminating background information: "In the ancient world both governments and individuals kept records of populations. These records were used for many of the same sorts of purposes that official records are used for in modern times—taxation, military duty, establishing property ownership."[7]

When we turn to the last book of the Bible we find that two books are in view. The first is the book of deeds or works. "On the day of final judgment the book of deeds will be opened, and each person will be judged according to what he or she has done."[8] John the apostle describes the scene: "And the sea gave up the dead who were in it, Death and Hades gave up the dead who were in them, and they were judged, each one of them, according to what they had done"(Rev. 20:13). Being judged for what one has done reveals that retributive justice is the operating principle of divine judgment. This is the common view in the Old and New Testaments (e.g., Ps. 62:12; Prov. 24:12; Rom. 2:6; 2 Cor. 5:10; Col. 3:25; 1 Pet. 1:17). David Penchansky rightly observes: "Retribution means that God gives to individuals and

7. Douglas K. Stuart, *Exodus*, The New American Commentary (Nashville: Broadman & Holman, 2006), 685.
8. Leland Ryken et al., *Dictionary of Biblical Imagery* (Downers Grove, IL: InterVarsity Press, 2000), 114.

communities a degree of suffering that somehow corresponds to their sin and offense. The idea of retribution serves as the cornerstone for the central theological claim that God governs the world with justice."[9]

The book of deeds is not the only book mentioned in Revelation. John writes: "The beast that you saw was, and is not, and is about to rise from the bottomless pit and go to destruction. And the dwellers on earth whose names have not been written in the book of life from the foundation of the world will marvel to see the beast, because it was and is not and is to come"(Rev. 17:8). The ownership of the book becomes clear in Revelation 21:27: "But nothing unclean will ever enter it, nor anyone who does what is detestable or false, but only those who are written in the Lamb's book of life." Those written there Jesus will acknowledge before his heavenly Father.[10]

Union with Christ: The Key

The early church fathers believed that where the head goes, the body will follow. They saw this in the birth of a baby: first comes the head and then the body. Thomas F. Torrance develops this early church idea: "Now Christ the Head of the Body is already resurrected, the First-born of the New Creation, and as such he is the pledge and guarantee that we who are incorporated with him as his Body will rise with him and be born into new creation in our physical as well as spiritual existence."[11]

Calvin, too, knew the importance of our incorporation into Christ. In his discussion of the benefits Christ brings and our relation to them, he argues:

9. David Penchansky, "Retribution," in *The New Interpreter's Dictionary of the Bible*, ed. Katharine Doob Sakenfeld, 5 vols. (Nashville: Abingdon, 2000), 4:781.

10. Penchansky, "Retribution," 781.

11. Thomas F. Torrance, *Space, Time and Resurrection* (Grand Rapids, MI: Eerdmans, 1976), 142. Torrance cites Irenaeus as an example of a church father holding this view.

We must now examine this question. How do we receive those benefits which the Father bestowed on his only-begotten Son—not for Christ's own private use, but that he might enrich poor and needy men? First, we must understand that as long as Christ remains outside of us, and we are separated from him, all that he has suffered and done for the salvation of the human race remains useless and of no value for us. Therefore, to share with us what he has received from the Father, he had to become ours and to dwell within us. For this reason, he is called "our Head" [Eph. 4:15], and "the first-born among many brethren" [Rom. 8:29]. We also, in turn, are said to be "engrafted into him" [Rom. 11:17], and to "put on Christ" [Gal. 3:27]; for, as I have said, all that he possesses is nothing to us until we grow into one body with him. It is true that we obtain this by faith.[12]

In Calvin's theology this union is brought about not by the sacraments (contra Rome) but by the secret work of the Holy Spirit.[13]

Christ has gone to glory, and so will we go to glory in union with him. No other creature has such a destiny, not even angels. No other creature in heaven or earth is so privileged.

It Matters

Doing great things for God can be a heady experience, especially in a culture that prizes celebrity. Jesus's disciples, seventy-

---

12. John Calvin, *Institutes of the Christian Religion*, ed. John T. McNeill, trans. Ford Lewis Battles (Philadelphia: Westminster, 1960), 3.1.1.

13. According to Catholic doctrine, our union with Christ begins with baptism, is strengthened by confirmation, and is fed in the Eucharist. Through such sacraments we share in the divine nature. See Peter J. Kreeft, *Catholic Christianity: A Complete Catechism of Catholic Beliefs Based on the Catechism of the Catholic Church* (San Francisco: Ignatius, 2001), 302. In his argument with the Catholic Church of his day, Calvin rightly and persuasively argued from Scripture and not tradition. A hermeneutical rule of thumb would be to ask, Would the New Testament lead me to expect X or Y or Z? The New Testament leads me to expect the active role of the Holy Spirit in my union with Christ (see, e.g., 1 Cor. 12:12–13) but not the elaborate apparatus of the seven sacraments of Catholic teaching.

two of them, had a heady experience in the mission on which Jesus sent them: "The seventy-two returned with joy, saying, 'Lord, even the demons are subject to us in your name!' And he said to them, 'I saw Satan fall like lightning from heaven. Behold, I have given you authority to tread on serpents and scorpions, and over all the power of the enemy, and nothing shall hurt you'" (Luke 10:17–19). A great victory over evil ensued, and yet the disciples needed to get their perspective straightened out by Jesus: "Nevertheless, do not rejoice in this, that the spirits are subject to you, but rejoice that your names are written in heaven" (Luke 10:20). Sadly, one can do great things for God but for the wrong reason. Jesus warned in the Sermon on the Mount that on the last day there will be those who claim to belong to Jesus as Lord because of their deeds done in Jesus's name. These deeds include prophesying, exorcisms, and miracles. However, Jesus does not recognize all who do them as his (Matt. 7:21–23). The most poignant example of this awful possibility is Judas. He knew how to exorcize and do mighty works, but he also knew how to betray and so became "the son of destruction" (John 17:12).[14]

Who Will Not Be Glorified?

As we have seen, the new Jerusalem is glorious, and God's people will populate it, but what about those who do not belong?[15] The book of Revelation provides graphic descriptions of their fate. At a great white throne, there will be judgment according to works and the lake of fire: "And the sea gave up the dead who were in

14. "Destruction" in this reference most probably has Judas's future in mind. See D. A. Carson, *The Gospel according to John* (Leicester: Inter-Varsity Press; Grand Rapids, MI: Eerdmans, 1991), 563.

15. The fact that inscribed on the gates of the new Jerusalem are the twelve "names of the twelve tribes of the sons of Israel" and on the twelve foundations could be found "the twelve names of the twelve apostles of the Lamb" suggests that the population of the city of God includes the regenerate of both the old and new covenants (Rev. 21:12, 14).

it, Death and Hades gave up the dead who were in them, and they were judged, each one of them, according to what they had done. Then Death and Hades were thrown into the lake of fire. This is the second death, the lake of fire" (20:13–14). Furthermore, we read, "And if anyone's name was not found written in the book of life, he was thrown into the lake of fire" (20:15). This means exclusion from the divine presence as a result of the divine exercise of retributive justice. Those so excluded become outsiders: "But as for the cowardly, the faithless, the detestable, as for murderers, the sexually immoral, sorcerers, idolaters, and all liars, their portion will be in the lake that burns with fire and sulfur, which is the second death" (21:8). Revelation 22:15 is striking: "Outside are the dogs and sorcerers and the sexually immoral and murderers and idolaters, and everyone who loves and practices falsehood."[16] In a morally serious universe, judgment is essential. The timing of it is in the divine Judge's keeping.

This is not the destiny of those found in the Lamb's book of life: "But nothing unclean will ever enter it, nor anyone who does what is detestable or false, but only those who are written in the Lamb's book of life" (21:27). Those in the Lamb's book of life have access to the city of God and the tree of life. The exclusion described in Genesis 3:24 has become the embrace of Revelation 22:14: "Blessed are those who wash their robes, so that they may have the right to the tree of life and that they may enter the city by the gates."

What Sort of Body Will the Excluded Have?

Just what would embodied existence look like for those excluded from the divine presence? It is an interesting question.

---

16. Edward Arthur Litton suggests that the presence of such outsiders may indicate that those who belong to the Lamb may be in for "active service, arduous duty—even conflict with evil." *Introduction to Dogmatic Theology* (London: James Clarke, 1960), 605. However, this is hardly correct, given the finality that Rev. 20:15 presents.

However, we need to distinguish carefully between convictions biblically anchored, opinions that are less so, and speculations that have little anchorage in the biblical testimony, even if, in the end, some may turn out to be true.

It has been said that the philosopher for the Orthodox is Plato, for the Catholics is Aristotle, and for the Protestants is Augustine. I would add that for many evangelicals it is C. S. Lewis. Lewis turned his imagination to the afterlife and the nature of existence in *The Great Divorce*.[17] He used the idea of solidity to describe the difference between the saved and the lost. On the one hand, the saved become more and more substantial in the world to come. The lost, on the other hand, become less and less substantial, until they fade away.

It may seem odd to discuss Lewis in a work like this. However, he has had a great deal of influence upon evangelical scholars and theologians. N. T. Wright is a case in point. Wright rejects both universalism and annihilationism.[18] So, what does Wright propose? On this topic of the fate of those excluded, Wright acknowledges that he is speculating about "one of the darkest theological mysteries."[19] He proposes a third way: "When human beings give their heartfelt allegiance to and worship that which is not God, they progressively cease to reflect the image of God." What's the consequence? Wright offers the following speculation:

> My suggestion is that it is possible for human beings so to continue down this road, so to refuse all whisperings of

17. C. S. Lewis, *The Great Divorce* (Glasgow: Collins, 1972).

18. Universalists argue that all will be saved in the end. The annihilationist maintains that after experiencing hell for a certain period of time, the lost will cease to exist. The duration of their conscious punishment will be commensurate with the gravity of each individual's sin. For a critical discussion of both positions, see Paul R. Williamson, *Death and the Afterlife: Biblical Perspectives on Ultimate Questions* (Downers Grove, IL: IVP Academic, 2018), passim.

19. Wright, *Surprised by Hope*, 183.

good news, all glimmers of the true light, all promptings to turn and go the other way, all signposts of the love of God, that after death they become at last, by their own affective choice, *beings that once were human but now are not*, creatures that have ceased to bear the divine image at all. . . . They pass simultaneously not only beyond hope but also beyond pity.[20]

According to Wright, such creatures "still exist in an ex-human state."

Wright is to be applauded for characterizing his ruminations as speculation. Not all theologians are that careful. Even so, speculation it is. His view begs the question whether such creatures are still conscious of their wrongdoing and their punishment. All the details in the parable Jesus told about the rich man and Lazarus are not to be overly pressed. It is, after all, a parable (Luke 16:19–31). However, the story does assume that the rich man is conscious and in torment. And there is no hint that he is becoming increasingly subhuman. He remains a speech agent who can say "I" throughout the story.[21]

An Intriguing Suggestion

G. Campbell Morgan (1863–1945) was a great preacher of an earlier era. Many of his works are still in print. He argued that the Scriptures offer three definitive statements about the divine nature: God is light, God is love, and God is a consuming fire.[22] And the God who is a consuming fire is present even in hell, not only in heaven. After all, God is omnipresent. Morgan speculated, "Hell and heaven are one in atmosphere, and the

---

20. Wright, *Surprised by Hope*, 182, original emphasis.

21. In conversation with me, the New Testament scholar D. A. Carson observed that the rich man gives no hint of consciousness that his torment is just.

22. G. Campbell Morgan, *The Westminster Pulpit*, vol. 1, *The Preaching of G. Campbell Morgan* (Eugene, OR: Wipf and Stock, 2012), 62.

atmosphere is burning, blistering pain, or a shining, beauteous glory, according to what I am."[23] His point is an interesting one. If the glorified partake of the divine nature, as 2 Peter 1:4 states, then the glorified will be fire like God in some unimaginable sense. But for the wicked that same fire is horrendous, because they do not partake of the divine nature. So for them the presence of the God who is fire is hellish.

However, Scripture needs to be compared with Scripture. That Scripture interprets Scripture is a fundamental of an evangelical hermeneutic. So the question must be asked as to how this intriguing suggestion fits with Jesus's declaring to the disobedient in the Sermon on the Mount "Depart from me, you workers of lawlessness" (Matt. 7:23). Likewise, how does Morgan's suggestion fit with Paul's description of judgment day in 2 Thessalonians 1:7–10?

> . . . when the Lord Jesus is revealed from heaven with his mighty angels in flaming fire, inflicting vengeance on those who do not know God and on those who do not obey the gospel of our Lord Jesus. They will suffer the punishment of eternal destruction, away from the presence of the Lord and from the glory of his might, when he comes on that day to be glorified in his saints, and to be marveled at among all who have believed, because our testimony to you was believed.

For the apostle, judgment means separation from the divine presence and from the divine glory. The glorified saints and the excluded don't appear to share the same environment at all.

What of Those Who Have Never Heard?

A common question is What about those who have not heard the gospel? Is there no hope of glorification for those not in a

---

23. Morgan, *Westminster Pulpit*, 68.

position to hear the good news of Jesus Christ? My own view is that we know from Scripture that those who hear and trust will be glorified. I find it hard to imagine that Christ can lose members of his own body or have God's children plucked from his hand (John 10:27–29).[24] The Scriptures don't entertain the question about those who have never heard the gospel. I think the reason for this is simple. It is a speculative question. The question arises only if one *has* heard. When Jesus was confronted with speculative questions, he turned them into existential ones. Luke 13:1–5 says:

> There were some present at that very time who told him about the Galileans whose blood Pilate had mingled with their sacrifices. And he answered them, "Do you think that these Galileans were worse sinners than all the other Galileans, because they suffered in this way? No, I tell you; but unless you repent, you will all likewise perish. Or those eighteen on whom the tower in Siloam fell and killed them: do you think that they were worse offenders than all the others who lived in Jerusalem? No, I tell you; but unless you repent, you will all likewise perish."

In practice, that means we evangelize and follow the apostolic desire: "Him we proclaim, warning everyone and teaching everyone with all wisdom, that we may present everyone mature in Christ. For this I toil, struggling with all his energy that he powerfully works within me" (Col. 1:28–29).

What is important to observe is that nowhere in Scripture are human beings judged for not responding to a Christ of whom they have never heard. Revelation 21 and 22 list concrete sinful behaviors from which exclusion from the divine presence

---

24. I affirm the eternal security of the children of God. Not all Bible believing scholars would agree. On the Arminian view, one's salvation may be lost. However, to my mind this turns a glorious salvation into probation.

results. Revelation 21:8 mentions "the cowardly, the faithless, the detestable, . . . murderers, the sexually immoral, sorcerers, idolaters, and all liars." Revelation 21:27 refers to anyone who does what is detestable or false. Revelation 22:15 lists "sorcerers and the sexually immoral and murderers and idolaters, and everyone who loves and practices falsehood." The apostle Paul also lists concrete behaviors when he writes to the Corinthians: "Do you not know that the unrighteous will not inherit the kingdom of God? Do not be deceived: neither the sexually immoral, nor idolaters, nor adulterers, nor men who practice homosexuality, nor thieves, nor the greedy, nor drunkards, nor revilers, nor swindlers will inherit the kingdom of God" (1 Cor. 6:9). Wonderfully, the gospel has taken root in this congregation despite all its troubles, so he goes on to draw the contrast: "And such were some of you. But you were washed, you were sanctified, you were justified in the name of the Lord Jesus Christ and by the Spirit of our God" (1 Cor. 6:11).

For those who have heard, unbelief looms large as the problem. For with unbelief comes disobedience. The failure of Adam and Eve was not to trust in the goodness of God who had provided a paradise for them (Gen. 3:1–7). This unbelief took the form of distrusting the word of God about not eating the fruit of the tree of the knowledge of good and evil, for death would ensue (Gen. 2:16–17). D. B. Knox correctly sums up the primal situation: "The problem Adam faced was, could God be trusted?"[25] Our first parents were tempted by that great spoiler, the devil, to doubt the goodness of God.[26] Unbelief in the word of God is eternally fatal. Revelation 20 terms it the second death (v. 14).

---

25. D. B. Knox, *Justification by Faith* (London: Church Book Room, 1959), 9.
26. For more on the sin of unbelief in the word of God, see Graham A. Cole, *God the Peacemaker: How Atonement Brings Shalom* (Downers Grove, IL: InterVarsity Press, 2009), 58–60.

Conclusion

The glorified are those in union with Christ. They are the population of the new Jerusalem. They have access to the tree of life because their names are in the Lamb's book of life. They are embraced.

However, there is another population. These are those whose unforgiven behavior excludes them from the divine presence. The lake of fire is their destiny. This is an awful prospect. Both the glorified and the excluded are embodied. Speculating about the kind of embodiment they have is just that, speculation. What is clear is that this a morally serious universe in which creatures (we and angels) will be accountable.

Conclusion

"The best is yet to be," indeed, as the Christian poet Robert Browning wrote.[1] God has a project. He is restoring his defaced images to the likeness of Christ. The kingly vocation which Adam lost is restored by Christ, the new Adam. Those who have been saved by Christ will become glorified beings of exalted status as coheirs and corulers with him. Our coming glorification has ontological, epistemological, and vocational aspects.

But do we live like this is so? Or do we live with a spiritually debilitating, shrunken eschatological horizon? The heavenly state is penultimate, not ultimate. The new heavens and new earth are the ultimate.

Years ago, I was conversing with an Old Testament scholar, Francis Anderson. By then, in retirement, he was teaching as an adjunct. I knew that he had been ill, so I asked him, "Frank, how are you?" He replied, "Nothing that a good resurrection would not fix." Resurrection is part of what Frank had to look forward to. Glorification is the summit. Anthony Thiselton explains why that prospect is the summit: "The 'glory' which awaits every Christian is precisely and primarily the presence of God.'"[2]

---

1. Robert Browning, "Rabbi Ben Ezra," Poetry Foundation, https://www.poetry foundation.org/, accessed May 8, 2020.

2. Anthony C. Thiselton, *Life after Death: A New Approach to the Last Things* (Grand Rapids, MI: Eerdmans, 2012), 185.

Glorification won't be the destiny of every child of Adam. Glorification is for those who are redeemed in union with Christ by his Spirit. The glorification process begins in this age. That is to say, it is for those who are in Christ. In the age to come, the believer's glorified body will be like that of the risen Christ. So much about this prospect is unimaginable. In this life it is a matter of faith, not sight. Indeed, in this life the outer nature wastes away while the inner nature is being renewed daily, as the apostle Paul has taught us. For those who remain in Adam, there is no glory to come. Hell is real. Embodiment continues in some form for believer and unbeliever alike. But what that continued embodiment looks like exactly is a matter of some speculation. Speculations have their place in Christian thinking, but no doctrine should be built on them, even if they come from someone with the reputation of C. S. Lewis.

In doctrinal perspective, the glorification theme shows the interlocking of a number of important doctrines. Theological anthropology is involved, as it is our embodied humanity that is glorified. Christology is involved, because Christ's glorification is the template for our own. Pneumatology is involved, because the Spirit is the agent of transformation. Indeed, the Trinity is involved: the Father as the architect of our glorification, the Son as the pattern, and the Holy Spirit as the one who effects and perfects change. Soteriology is involved, because our glorification is a great benefit of the gospel. Eschatology is involved, having individual, corporate, and cosmic aspects. The doctrine of glorification especially concentrates on the individual, but even so, the corporate and cosmic dimensions are not to be lost to sight. The glorified have a new cosmos to enjoy, and do so with others. The new heavens and the new earth are the setting for glorified beings, plural.

Most importantly, our hoped-for glorification rests on the promise of a good and almighty God who wants us in his glorious presence, and only a glorified creature is fit for such divine company.

Further Reading

Gomes, Alan W. *40 Questions about Heaven and Hell.* Grand Rapids, MI: Kregel Academic, 2018. A most helpful book in a fine series of useful books. Chapters 19 and 20 are especially relevant.

Jacob, Haley Goranson. *Conformed to the Image of His Son: Reconsidering Paul's Theology of Glory in Romans.* Downers Grove, IL: IVP Academic, 2018. A challenging read for those without knowledge of Greek or Hebrew, but a seminal work.

Moore, Russell D. "Personal and Cosmic Eschatology." In *A Theology for the Church*, edited by Daniel L. Akin, 671–722. Rev. ed. Nashville: B&H, 2014. An outstanding essay in a most helpful one-volume systematic theology.

Morgan, Christopher W., and Robert A. Peterson, eds. *The Glory of God.* Wheaton, IL: Crossway, 2010. An excellent treatment of the theme of divine glory by many fine scholars.

Morgan, Christopher W., and Robert A. Peterson, eds. *Heaven.* Wheaton, IL: Crossway, 2014. Another excellent treatment of the theme of divine glory by a cavalcade of fine scholars. Chapter 11 is especially relevant.

Ramm, Bernard. *Them He Glorified: A Systematic Study of the Doctrine of Glorification.* Grand Rapids, MI: Eerdmans, 1963. A pioneering evangelical exploration of the doctrine. Brief but worthwhile.

Smith, Ian K. *Not Home Yet: How the Renewal of the Earth Fits into God's Plan for the World*. Wheaton, IL: Crossway, 2019. A very helpful big-picture approach to the Christian hope.

Thiselton, Anthony C. *Life after Death: A New Approach to the Last Things*. Grand Rapids, MI: Eerdmans, 2012. A deep book written by a philosopher-theologian of note.

General Index

Scripture Index

Short Studies in Systematic Theology

For more information, visit **crossway.org**.